Blood of Nosferatu: A Play In Two Acts

Darryl Pickett

Published by Odsmil Press, 2022.

Revised Edition – First Printing

While every precaution has been taken in the preparation of this book, the publisher assumes no responsibility for errors or omissions, or for damages resulting from the use of the information contained herein.

BLOOD OF NOSFERATU: A PLAY IN TWO ACTS

First edition. October 15, 2022.

Copyright © 2022 Darryl Pickett.

ISBN: 979-8215399958

Written by Darryl Pickett.

Table of Contents

For Debbie Butcher

(My favorite vampire fan)

Dramatis Personae

This revision premiered on Oct. 29th, 2019, presented by the Enniscorthy Drama Group at The Presentation Centre, Enniscorthy, Ireland, under the direction of Tom Reddy. The play requires a cast of sixteen performers, traditionally 8 male, 6 female, and 2 children, male and female. (non-traditional casting in regards to race and gender has also been successful) In order of appearance:

Dr. Jack Seward - *A specialist* - *John Kerwin*

Professor Abraham Van Helsing - *A scientist* - *Richie Cotter*

Mina Murray - *fiance of Jonathan Harker* - *Hannah McNiven*

Jonathan Harker – *A solicitor* - *Alan Kinsella*

Thomas Renfield - *A patient* - *Pat Murphy*

Count Dracula - *Ancient warrior* - Ronan P. Byrne

Lucy Westenra - *Mina's closest friend* - Kate Breen

Miriam Westenra – *Mother of Lucy* - Jennifer Boyd

Father Shaugnessy - *A priest* - Peter Canning

Arthur Holmwood/ Lord Godalming - *Recent heir to the title* - Murt Murphy

Quincy Morris - *American industrialist.* - Jer Ennis

The Vampire Brides:

Karena - Julie Fox

Anja - Karen Franklin

Katja - Laura Franklin

The Children:

Harriet - *Missing girl, around 10* - Maeve Ennis

Simon/Sally – *Younger sibling, about 6* - Jennifer Kelly

The performers For Arthur Holmwood and Quincy may double for the roles of **Jenkins** *and* **Parsons,** *attendees at Van Helsing's lecture at the beginning of Act One.*

Act One

<hr>

Prelude:

As soon as the house is open, a mood of foreboding and dread is established. RENFIELD sits on a single chair mid-stage, confined in a straight jacket. For a long time, he only sits, staring into the middle distance, seemingly catatonic. After a while, his expression animates, as if responding to a voice inside his consciousness. Eerie sounds and music gradually escalate in intensity. During this time, Renfield strains and struggles until he has escaped from the straight jacket. With a cunning smile, he makes his way off stage. Silence follows.

1-1: A Lecture Hall

SOUND: *Voices of students and colleagues chattering as they enter the hall. VAN HELSING sits on the single chair. DR. JACK SEWARD steps to the platform and gestures the crowd to settle down. He speaks just a bit nervously to the crowd.*

SEWARD - Good afternoon. I am pleased that so many were able to attend. I am Doctor Jack Seward. I'd like to welcome you to the final set of lectures in our series on metaphysics and the paranormal. In our field of psychological care, it is good to consider these possibilities, no matter how unconventional they may seem. Our guest today is Abraham Van Helsing. He's a longtime friend of the Institute, and a protege of our own Dr. Arminius. And now, I entreat you to keep an open mind as you welcome Professor Abraham Van Helsing.

Seward steps aside and moves into the house as ABRAHAM VAN HELSING stands to take the stage. He is an impressive, stern-faced man with a commanding presence. JENKINS and PARSONS stand in the house, at either side of the audience.

VAN HELSING - Thank you, Dr. Seward. *Vampires!* Can any of you tell me that there are no such things? I do not think so. That vampires exist, I have absolutely no doubt. I hope to demonstrate for you my reasons. But let me be very careful to make distinctions. When I say vampire, do I mean the creatures that populate cheap fiction and the stage of the Grand Guignol? No, I do not. I am talking about a real and scientifically verifiable phenomenon.

JENKINS - *(from the house)* - I'm sorry, Dr. Seward, but I cannot sit and listen to this!

SEWARD - Please, Mr. Jenkins. I beg you.

JENKINS - Is he really going to tell us that there are undead creatures who drink the blood of the living?

VAN HELSING - Yes! This is factual. There exist creatures that drink human blood.

PARSONS - *(also from the house)* So, a kind of cannibal then?

VAN HELSING - There are madmen who engage in such perverse acts of blood lust. But that is not what I mean. It is hard to separate fact from myth, young man. I do draw a distinction between a true vampire and a simple bloodthirsty madman. Now, tell me, what do you know about vampires?

PARSONS - They cast no reflection.

VAN HELSING - That is a myth, my friend. According to legend, the vampire is a creature without a soul, and therefore it has neither shadow nor reflection. But does this make rational sense?

PARSONS - It is conjectural, Professor, but I see no way to prove or disprove it.

VAN HELSING - Mr....ah...

PARSONS - Parsons, sir.

VAN HELSING - Mr. Parsons, tell me something. Do you have a mirror in your dormitory?

PARSONS - Yes sir.

VAN HELSING - And you do cast a reflection in it, yes?

PARSONS - Of course

VAN HELSING - And your dresser, your bed, your worktable, you see these in the mirror too, right?

PARSONS - Yes.

VAN HELSING - Do you conjecture, then, that your bed, your dresser and your table possess a soul, Mr. Parsons?

PARSONS - No, sir.

VAN HELSING - Of course not. So, I think that we can reasonably conclude that physical objects, living and otherwise, cast a reflection, regardless of whether or not they have a soul, right?

PARSONS - Yes, Professor.

VAN HELSING - A little more intellectual rigor is required of you. We must not fall into romanticized ideas, however they may engage the popular fancy. Our job is to ask hard questions and seek the truth diligently. Now, any other myths we might examine?

JENKINS - That they fear the holy cross.

VAN HELSING - Ah yes. Well, what is your guess? Is this likely to be true?

JENKINS - I suppose it might be, if the vampire in question is Catholic.

Sound: Laughter from crowd

VAN HELSING - You may laugh, but this is a fine observation. A vampire might well shrink from the holy cross if convinced of its power. But what if our vampire is not?

JENKINS - Then this would only be true if the cross actually carried an innate power of its own.

VAN HELSING - And does it?

JENKINS - I scarcely know, sir.

VAN HELSING - Vampires are intelligent beings, and thus also capable of holding to the superstitions of their own culture. But make no mistake. They are the undead. They require blood to retain their horrible non-life. They are animal beings. They can be destroyed but it is no easy task.

JENKINS - Have *you* ever killed a vampire, Professor?

BLOOD OF NOSFERATU: A PLAY IN TWO ACTS

VAN HELSING - *(hesitant at first)* I have been present at the destruction of a vampire. It must be found by daylight where it sleeps. It must be drained of blood. It must be decapitated.

SEWARD - This is hard to accept, Van Helsing.. I'm a man of science.

Van Helsing - And so am I. This is fact. A corpse can return to life. I have witnessed such ghastly resurrections, now several times. The vampire selects a victim to join the ranks of the undead. This person's blood is drained away, and replaced by the infected blood of the vampire. This new blood carries with it a sort of disease, like a plague. The victim develops symptoms, weakens and dies. Yes, *all* life functions have ceased! And then, over a period of days, the transformation takes place. The muscles begin to move. The heart beats again. The body rises and walks, and hunts!

Sound: A cacophony of yelling and objections from the assembly.

Van Helsing leaves the platform as the sound fades. Seward and the others exit as well

1-2: A Hotel Boudoir

―――

The box on the upper platform is turned short side out, and covered to represent a bed. MINA and JONATHAN sit on the bed. As the lights rise, they are engaged in a passionate lover's kiss. Their exchange reflects the comfortable and intimate nature of their relationship.

MINA - Will you miss me?

HARKER - Silly question.

MINA - I know. I feel silly asking it.

HARKER - Good.

MINA - But will you?

HARKER - *(amused)* It will be agony.

MINA - Thank you.

HARKER - Are you all right?

MINA - I'm sad that you're leaving.

HARKER - I won't be gone two weeks.

MINA - Long enough.

HARKER - Are you sure that's all? You seem strange.

MINA - *(after a sigh and a pause)* I was arrested.

HARKER - Again. When and where?

MINA - Last week, in Birmingham. I was charged with inciting a riot. Why are you smiling?

HARKER - Because I'm pleased! Were you talking suffrage?

MINA - I wasn't talking. I was shouting. Everyone was shouting. Anyway, I was only put in gaol for an hour. Long enough to be made an example. The papers were there. Word will surely reach London by the time I get back. I am trouble, Jonathan. I will always be trouble.

HARKER - I know. That's why I fell in love with you.

MINA - Your employers won't like it.

HARKER - My employers have no say in the matter. It's not high treason to speak out. Even Parliament has its advocates for equality.

MINA - Advocates who are men. They get to say what they like. But such talk isn't to be entertained coming from the mouth of a woman.

HARKER - Well, not from a woman like you, no.

MINA - What do you mean?

HARKER - Well, suffragettes are supposed to be homely. Beaky old spinsters, rotund governesses. Stern faced matrons. But you? You're too pretty. You're meant to be the blushing bride, the gentle, nurturing mother, the embodiment of the domestic goddess. I'm not saying I follow this line of thought...

MINA - (*moving closer to Jonathan*) I'm not a goddess to you?

HARKER - Well, to *me*, yes.

MINA - You're completely silly.

HARKER - True. Seriousness of thought has never been a strength. Come to think of it, what are my strong points? You can't be after my money. I haven't got any.

MINA - Yet.

HARKER - And you can't be attracted to my hidebound political views.

MINA - I wouldn't call you hidebound. You're practically moderate.

HARKER - We'll see what marriage to you makes of me.

MINA - I promise I won't corrupt you too much.

They kiss again, very tenderly.

HARKER - Two weeks, and I'll be back in London.

MINA - I know.

HARKER - I will think of you every moment.

MINA - I know.

HARKER - And Mina.

MINA - Yes?

HARKER - Try to stay out of prison until after I get back.

1-3: The Lecture Hall

There is now a man sitting in the chair. This is RENFIELD. He is a small, meek looking man. He sits quietly, staring while idly twiddling his thumbs.

VAN HELSING - I thank you all for allowing me to return. What I have to say today relates to your own profession. You know already that the human mind can be misled. Our conscious brains show us things that are not there. This is important, because the vampire possesses a power to manipulate the minds of its victims. It is because of this ability that a vampire is said to transform into a mist, a bat or a wolf. These are illusions, generated by the vampire's force of persuasion. This much we can understand and guard against.

Van Helsing turns his attention to Renfield. He takes from his pocket a metallic disc on a chain.

VAN HELSING - I have been given permission to place this subject under hypnosis. He is in a trance state right now. I shall place into his mind suggestions, harmless suggestions. At my prompting, he can engage in normal rational discourse. Sir, would you please give everyone your name?

RENFIELD - I am Thomas Renfield.

VAN HELSING - Will you please tell us your occupation?

RENFIELD - I am an apprentice bookbinder.

VAN HELSING - I see. Have you ever before been placed into the hypnotic state?

RENFIELD - Only once, when we met at your office. You made me sleep.

VAN HELSING - That is right. I put you into a mild trance. Did you experience any discomfort?

RENFIELD - None.

VAN HELSING - Any fear or apprehension?

RENFIELD - Not a bit.

VAN HELSING - This is good. Please make yourself as comfortable as you can.

Van Helsing swings the medallion in front of Renfield's eyes for a moment.

VAN HELSING - Please close your eyes. You will now be in a pleasant state of rest.

Van Helsing picks up a small dish, on which are cut sections of an apple.

VAN HELSING - *(to audience)* Now, before I bring Mr. Renfield back to full consciousness, I wish to show you that I have a portion of sliced apple, bought from a vendor just outside. Mr. Renfield, I will ask you to taste something. It will seem to you to be a portion of roast beef. It will be tender, warm and delicious. Now, Mr. Renfield, I will count to three, at which time you will open your eyes. You will feel as though you are completely awake and refreshed. One...two...three... (*He snaps his fingers and Renfield comes to.*) Hello, Mr. Renfield. Are you feeling well?

RENFIELD - I feel fine.

VAN HELSING - You have been asleep. Were you aware of this?

RENFIELD - No sir. I've just been answering your questions, haven't I?

VAN HELSING - I am wondering, Mr. Renfield, if you are feeling hungry.

RENFIELD - A little bit, yes.

VAN HELSING - I would like you to try this roast beef.

He proffers the plate to Renfield, who receives it politely.

RENFIELD - I don't care all that much for beef. I'll eat it if it will please you.

VAN HELSING - Go ahead, please, Mr. Renfield. Could you describe to us how it tastes?

RENFIELD - It's a bit overdone, a little dry. I prefer it nice and bloody, you see.

VAN HELSING - Are you certain that it is beef?

RENFIELD - Quite certain. Not a fine cut, mind you. A little tough.

VAN HELSING - (*taking the plate*) Thank you, Mr. Renfield. When I count to three, you will resume your sleep. One...two...three...

Renfield quickly returns to unconsciousness. Van Helsing picks up a small box, opens it, and puts onto a plate an astonishing specimen of beetle.

VAN HELSING - I now wish to show the limits of suggestion. It is one thing to eat an apple under the pretense that it is roast beef. It's quite another to offer something repulsive. I have here a specimen from our laboratory, a very large species of beetle from the African continent. This particular bug is alive, harmless but intimidating. The subject is likely to recognize the extreme nature of the stimulus. Mr. Renfield, what I am about to give you will seem to be a most pleasant sweetmeat, of a kind you have always favored. Awaken on the count of three, Mr. Renfield. One...two...three...

Renfield is again alert.

Van Helsing - Mr. Renfield, you are still feeling fine?

RENFIELD - Yes, better than ever.

VAN HELSING - I have here a treat, something very nice. Does this look appealing to you?

RENFIELD - Where did you find this? May I try it?

VAN HELSING - Are you sure you want to?

RENFIELD - With your permission ...(*he lifts it to his mouth and bites into it*) So much life...

VAN HELSING - No! Mr. Renfield, I beg you, please stop!

RENFIELD - But I have your permission!

VAN HELSING - On the count of three, please resume sleep, one...two...three... Mr. Renfield!

Renfield continues to consume the insect. Seward comes onto the stage to assist Van Helsing.

VAN HELSING - Dr. Seward, please help me take it from him!

RENFIELD - It's mine! You can't have it!

Seward gets hold of Rendfield's hands, but Renfield shoves him away. Van Helsing takes Renfield by the shoulder. Renfield lashes out violently at Van Helsing. Soon, the Professor is knocked down to his knees by the considerable strength of his subject.

RENFIELD - You bastard! You gave it to me! I must have blood! I must have life!

SEWARD - Attendants! Attendants!

RENFIELD - The blood is the life!

The lights dim as Seward and Van Helsing take Renfield by either shoulder and manage to take him off stage.

1-4: A Chamber at Castle Dracula

Harker, downstage, carrying a traveling case, speaks the words of a letter to Mina.

HARKER - May 19, 1897 – Dearest Mina, I am near the end of my journey. I have traveled alone through some of the strangest country imaginable. This evening, I arrive at the castle of my client, Count Dracula. My employers describe him as a gentleman of refinement. Yet everywhere I mention his name, from Budapest to Bistritz, I get the strangest reactions. There is superstition about the name. It seems to be connected with a curse. I carry no preconceptions. I look forward to meeting the Count. I hope he will be satisfied that all matters pertaining to Carfax Abbey have been well addressed.

Lights down on Harker.

Sound: Hoof beats and the rolling wheels of a stagecoach.

Lights up.

Shadows on the backdrop suggest an arched doorway. On the platform, an ornate but dilapidated chair. Harker enters and sets down his bag.

HARKER - Hello. Is anyone there? Hello!

The voice of COUNT DRACULA sounds from the darkness. Light slowly reveals a cloaked figure. Dracula remains in shadow, his face unseen. His voice is deep, even-tempered but commanding. For now, it cracks a bit with the roughened sound of old age. Sound: Distant echoes of creaks, wind and the sound of a fire in a fireplace.

DRACULA - Come in, Mr. Harker.

HARKER - Count Dracula?

DRACULA - Welcome to my ancient home. Please make yourself comfortable.

HARKER - I'm sorry, I cannot see you.

DRACULA - That is my wish for now. Sit, please. I trust your journey was agreeable.

HARKER - (*sitting*) Rustic. I'm not used to these ancient roads.

DRACULA - I did arrange for the coach that brought you here. When it is time for your return, it will take you back to Borgo Pass. I expect you are weary. I have arranged for your supper as well.

HARKER - Thank you.

Dracula emerges from the darkness and stands directly behind the chair. His face is still mostly in shadow.

DRACULA - Do you find the fire warm enough? The night will grow colder.

HARKER - I'm fine. I beg your pardon, Count, but it is disconcerting to speak to a voice with no face.

DRACULA - I am unwell, Mr. Harker. I beg your indulgence in this. You shall see me presently.

Harker attempts to look around at his host. Dracula gently but firmly turns his head back toward the fire. Harker immediately falls into a kind of trance.

DRACULA - Do not turn to look. Watch the fire. Let your body rest. You have traveled far, and now, you will sleep. You are in the arms of the sweet goddess of dreams.

1-5: Dr. Seward's Office at the Sanitarium

———

Lower stage, a side table and chair represent a small office. Seward and Van Helsing discuss their recent encounter with Renfield. Seward holds a file folder.

VAN HELSING - A volunteer who required sedation and confinement. Am I to understand, Dr. Seward, that you had previous knowledge of this man's instability.

SEWARD - I did not recognize him. But yes, he was a patient of mine. He was committed under the name Mark Stroeb. I had never heard of Thomas Renfield before, though even when he was our charge, he assumed a number of identities.

VAN HELSING - You released such a man?

SEWARD - He was transferred to another facility. We couldn't handle him. He was a master of escape. He got out four times in the three years he was here.

VAN HELSING - And now he returns voluntarily?

SEWARD - It's strange, Van Helsing. I can't believe I sat here with the two of you yesterday for half an hour and I never truly saw him. But as soon as he yelled the words "The blood is the life," I knew that it was Mark Stroeb. Those words were a kind of battle cry. He is diagnosed a zoophagous paranoid. He once told us that eating living creatures would allow him to consume their life force and prolong his own existence.

VAN HELSING - Yes. An intriguing delusion.

SEWARD - But if we are to treat him now, we must move carefully. Should he perceive us as friends, he may be amenable to this treatment you speak of. If not, well, you already know he is capable of violence.

A repentant looking Renfield enters the office

SEWARD - And here is the man of the hour.

RENFIELD - Dr. Seward. Professor Van Helsing.

VAN HELSING - Do I address you as Thomas Renfield?

RENFIELD - Of course.

VAN HELSING - Not as Mark Stroeb.

RENFIELD - No sir! That name belongs to a madman who once ruled my mind and body. He is no more. I killed him, starved him out of existence. I have abandoned the consumption of meat, you see. It wasn't until I ate that bit of roast beef that the infernal man inside of me reappeared. Oh, Dr. Seward, you must understand that I am, and always have been, Thomas Renfield. When you knew me before, you knew only a man possessed. I was born Thomas Renfield, and as that man, I am a normal and productive citizen.

SEWARD - How do you explain that attack upon poor Van Helsing?

RENFIELD - I regret it. I can only guess that somehow, this hypnotic spell of yours triggered it. (*Renfield falls to his knees in an obsequious display.*) Oh, Professor, please tell me this is what has happened! You will speak for me, won't you? I am not a lunatic. I am a simple and kindly man, with a wife and child. You must see how they would suffer if I were locked away.

SEWARD - It is not our intention to lock you up, Mr. Renfield. But I think that you require some observation, some testing.

VAN HELSING - *(To Renfield)* I think you may be right. The hypnotic process could have aroused this other person inside you. It is my belief that under hypnosis, that personality might forever be banished. I think I can cure you for good, Mr. Renfield, if you would agree to the treatment.

RENFIELD - Oh, Dr. Seward. Is what this man says possible? Is there hope that I might drive out that terrible man? I have dreams sometimes, terrible dreams about him.

SEWARD - All that remains is to keep you here at the hospital for one or two nights, under observation. If you suffer no relapse, you will be at complete liberty during treatment to go about your work and home life. Your cooperation speaks well to your chances for success.

RENFIELD - *(turning his unctuous attentions to Seward)* God bless you, Dr. Seward. You have saved my life. I cannot choose words fine enough to describe your compassion, your wisdom and generosity...

SEWARD - It's quite all right, Mr. Stroeb, er ... Mr. Renfield.

RENFIELD - I don't know how I will repay you, Doctor. But you'll see. I won't let you down. I will be an entirely new Thomas Renfield. You have my word.

1-6: The Chamber at Dracula's Castle

Two chairs are set on the upstage platform. They face each other at opposite ends, as if they define the ends of a table. Harker is slumped in the stage right chair. Dracula stands in semi-shadow behind the opposite chair.

DRACULA - Jonathan Harker!

HARKER - *(waking)* Oh! Have I been sleeping? I'm sorry.

DRACULA - Your journey has left you more weary than you imagined. *(He gestures at the space between them.)* As you can see, I have prepared a table for you.

HARKER - I feel a little faint.

DRACULA - It will pass. It is this climate. You are not adjusted to the thin air and the sharp cold. Food will make you stronger.

Dracula steps forward, revealing himself in full. He is an old man, tall and pale. His face, while human, has a bestial quality, somewhat wolf-like. His hair is long and white. There is both nobility in his bearing, and an otherworldly menace to his movement.

DRACULA - So, my young friend, you see your host at last. I hope my appearance does not frighten you. I am old and quite sick. But my health may soon improve. If I may say so, I feel much better now that you are here.

HARKER - *(standing)* Thank you. You are very kind. And you don't frighten me at all.

Harker sits back down, as if feeling faint. Dracula takes the opposite seat.

DRACULA - It is good of you to say so, but I think it must not be completely true. I hope that my table does not disappoint. I have no servants, and I subsist on very simple food.

HARKER - This is quite satisfactory, truly.

DRACULA - I keep many old customs. You have not lived as the ancient people lived.

HARKER - That's true enough. But, I hope to be broadened by the experience.

DRACULA - I hope to teach you much of the old ways. And you must tell me of the modern world. I have read in books of the wonders that man has brought about, but I have not seen them. And my speech, it is not that of the modern English gentleman.

HARKER - Your English is superior, Count, as far as I can determine.

DRACULA - You flatter me, young friend. I have already dined, but please enjoy. Because of my health, I must adhere to a limited diet. The right sustenance at the right time.

HARKER - This is good wine.

DRACULA - *Frauenblut*. It means "the virgin's blood." I am also fond of this wine.

HARKER - Won't you have any?

DRACULA - (*rising*) I must decline for the time being. My habits and my comings and goings may not make sense to you. My ways may seem strange, even alarming. My practices are perhaps more like the pagan than the Christian. I hope that you will not be troubled.

HARKER - Oh, I'm quite broadminded. As long as there aren't human sacrifices being carried out beneath my window.

DRACULA - I am not a savage, Mr. Harker.

HARKER - Oh, no. Of course not. I've been grossly impertinent. I'm sorry.

DRACULA - No need to apologize. I find your manner quite disarming. You have much of humor and good cheer about you. These are gifts of the young.

But please, attend to your supper, after which we may discuss the arrangements. You will tell me about my new home.

SOUND: the baying of wolves, not the lonely howl of a single animal, but the agitated song of an entire pack.

DRACULA - Do you hear that?

HARKER - Wolves?

DRACULA - The song of the children of darkness. Is their music pleasing to you?

HARKER - It's rather eerie.

DRACULA - They sing of the joy of the hunt, and the victory of the kill. Their prey must be fast and have their wits about them. They do not see in the dark, and so the wolf has the advantage. Where is their cleverness now? Where is their fleetness of foot? It is between the teeth of the wolf.

(lights fade)

1-7: A Parlor at the Westenra Home

Center stage: Revealed, three chairs and a small table set with tea service. LUCY WESTENRA tries to lend an arm to MIRIAM WESTENRA, late fifties and frail in body, though not in spirit. She holds a cane in one hand but moves steadily enough. FATHER SHAUGNESSY waits patiently near the door.

LUCY - Father Shaugnessy is here, Mother.

MIRIAM - Thank you, dear. I wish I hadn't slept so long.

LUCY - Please step carefully. Do you need my help?

MIRIAM - I require help from no one, Lucy. I can still walk. I may fall over dead in mid-step. But do not deny me the pleasure of making a proper thud in my final moment.

SHAUGNESSY - *(Stepping toward them)* Miriam. It's good to see that you are well.

MIRIAM - Oh, I am far from well, Father. But I am told that I'm improving. It's good of you to call.

SHAUGNESSY - It's been a long time. I only wish I had thought to call on you sooner.

MIRIAM - I have only recently returned from Manchester.

SHAUGNESSY - And how is your sister?

MIRIAM - *(surprised and confused)* She is dead, Father Shaugnessy.

SHAUGNESSY - Oh dear.

LUCY - Didn't you know?

SHAUGNESSY - I confess I didn't. Miriam, I am desolate. I can't begin to express my condolences.

Miriam chuckles.

LUCY - Are you all right, Mother?

MIRIAM - Quite. Forgive my impertinence, Father Shaugnessy. I had assumed that condolences were the purpose of your visit.

SHAUGNESSY - I meant to inquire after your health.

MIRIAM - I am living on the brink of annihilation. Oh, the doctors insist my recovery is strong and my health robust. And that is why I fear the worst. But tell me, Father, where have you been lately?

SHAUGNESSY - Birmingham. I was called to assist the vicar at St. Chad's.

LUCY - How lovely. I like Birmingham.

Mina enters the room, unseen by Shaugnessy.

SHAUGNESSY - So do I. Alas, the atmosphere was not always peaceful. There was a near riot last week.

LUCY - Oh my. I don't suppose it was Miss Murray's riot.

SHAUGNESSY - Mina Murray, yes. You know of her?

LUCY - She's staying with us.

SHAUGNESSY - Is she?

MINA - *(joining them)* I am, Father.

LUCY - Father Shaugnessy, I'd like you to meet my dear friend Mina Murray.

SHAUGNESSY - You are well known to me, Miss Murray.

MINA - I hope you don't think me a villain.

SHAUGNESSY - Heavens, no! I think you are very brave. It can't be easy to stand up for what you think is right.

MINA - Surely you do the same thing, Father. From the pulpit.

SHAUGNESSY - It is no act of bravery for me to preach official church doctrine. You champion a view with which many disagree.

MINA - Do you disagree, Father?

SHAUGNESSY - I must keep my own council, my dear. I will just say that you have given me rich food for thought.

MINA - *(to Lucy)* Has Arthur Holmwood arrived yet?

LUCY - I expect him any moment now.

MIRIAM - Then I shall have to receive him. Pity. Arthur is a frightful bore.

LUCY - He has come into his title. He is Lord Godalming.

MIRIAM - Oh, then Archibald has passed. He wore that title with grace. Dear Archibald Holmwood. You know, he wanted to marry me. And suppose I had. Young Arthur would never have been. But then, neither would young Lucy have been, and I wouldn't want that.

LUCY - Arthur is a gentleman. Perhaps he is a bit arrogant.

MIRIAM - To say the least. And what will you say to him when he proposes to you?

LUCY - What do you mean?

MIRIAM - It's why he's coming, my dear. Don't tell me you didn't know.

LUCY - Where did you get this idea...

ARTHUR HOLMWOOD and QUINCY MORRIS enter during the next line. Arthur is an aristocrat, well dressed and punctilious. Quincy is less refined, rugged and affable. Just now, he seems a little out of his element.

MIRIAM - Because he wrote to you about it. And if you're going to leave things where I can find them ... *(noticing the two arrivals)* Ah! Arthur, or, I suppose I must call you Lord Godalming.

ARTHUR - Miriam. You are looking well.

MIRIAM - Your father was a good man. I was fond of him.

ARTHUR - He spoke well of you, Miriam. And please allow me to express my deepest regrets at your recent loss.

MIRIAM - Of course. It's a sad time. But I thank you for your company.

ARTHUR - May I present to you Mr. Quincy Morris? He is my guest.

MIRIAM - Mr. Morris.

QUINCY - The honor is mine, Ma'am.

ARTHUR - Mister Morris is from the United States. Texas, actually. He is here on business, but we've struck up a fast friendship.

MIRIAM - Are you in industry, Mr. Morris?

QUINCY - Yes, Ma'am.

ARTHUR - Quincy is practically a legend in the States. He has fought in their war against the savages of the Apache tribe, and built his own fortune in textiles. A remarkable man.

QUINCY - Whoa, that's plenty, Lord Godalming. I can blow my own horn just fine. Lady Westenra, I'm not a man of refinement so forgive me if I say something ignorant from time to time. You're very gracious to have me.

MIRIAM - It's my pleasure. And I'm not a Lady. I'm just Mrs. Westenra. In fact, please call me Miriam. You know my daughter Lucy?

QUINCY - We've met. You gave birth to an angel, Miriam.

MIRIAM - That's true enough. And this is Father Shaugnessy, an ancient friend of the family. By which I don't mean to say that he himself is ancient.

SHAUGNESSY - I'm very nearly so.

MIRIAM - Well, don't we all make a fine party.

Mina clears her throat.

MIRIAM - Oh, I've nearly forgotten Mina. Have you met Quincy Morris?

MINA - Not yet. It's my pleasure, Mr. Morris.

QUINCY - I've heard all about you, Miss Murray.

MINA - From Lord Godalming? Well, that can't have been good.

MIRIAM - What do you mean, dear?

ARTHUR - Miss Murray no doubt alludes to a recent public dispute. Suffrage and fair wages. I fear my arguments were not always tempered with reason. Miss Murray, I wish to apologize for some of the remarks I made which you may have construed as demeaning.

MINA - *Some* of the remarks, Mr. Holmwood? I accept the apology while wondering which epithets still apply.

ARTHUR - It may interest you to know that in the intervening time, I have softened my view on suffrage. I now think that in time, our society may adapt to some reasonable compromise.

MINA - That's progress, at least.

QUINCY - Don't give him too much credit, Miss Murray. He didn't have any big change of heart. He just realized he's missing out on a great voting constituency.

ARTHUR - Thank you, Mr. Morris.

MINA - Before you know it, you'll be another John Stuart Mill.

QUINCY - Who's that?

ARTHUR - The author of *The Subjection of Women.*

MINA - You know of it?

ARTHUR - *(dryly)* I've read it.

SHAUGNESSY - Well, I do think we shall have some lively debate over supper!

MIRIAM - We will not, Father. I insist we be civil. Better than that. Let us be friends this night.

MINA -I'm sorry, Miriam. We forget ourselves.

MIRIAM - *(rising)* It's all right, my dear. We have an hour until the meal is served. I wish to rest until then. I trust you all to continue amicably without me.

Exit Miriam. All except Lucy and Mina exit after light change.

1-8: Lucy's Antechamber

Lucy sits in a downstage chair and unties the ribbon in her hair. Mina brushes Lucy's hair. Lucy gazes ahead, as if in a mirror.

LUCY - I remember when you were very fond of Arthur. When did your relationship become so strained?

MINA - I suppose it was last year. I was invited to his gentleman's club, for a summit on how to help the less fortunate. I wasn't allowed into any room except one small chamber where the meeting was held. His friends treated me with open scorn, and Arthur did nothing to defend me. I felt these men were treating me like a leper, and I said so. Arthur berated me for being ungracious. It became a war of words. In the end, they turned me out like a criminal. I must be something very frightening to them.

LUCY - But it isn't always so bad, is it? You keep saying the world is changing.

MINA - Very slowly. Dearest Lucy, you haven't yet tried to walk in that world. Every door that matters is closed to us.

LUCY - So how have you managed to do all the things you have done?

MINA - I've had to fight, with knowledge and determination.

LUCY - How can you stand to always be fighting?

MINA - I don't seek it out. There is no other choice.

LUCY - But there is. Look at me. Quiet Lucy Westenra, complacent and pliant, and not at all brave.

MINA - That isn't so, Lucy. You've shown tremendous strength during your mother's time of hardship. I know she would agree.

LUCY - I doubt it. She admires you, Mina. She must wish that I were as strong as you are. It seems all I can do is keep up this pretty, happy appearance. I'm a laughing ornament. Not much more.

MINA - Don't think that way. You can assert yourself. Speak what is on your mind. Be honest. There are people who will want to hear you.

LUCY - But will I have anything important to say?

MINA - Whatever is in your heart. And what *is* in your heart, Lucy? I mean, specifically, where Arthur Holmwood is concerned.

LUCY - He's an important man, and an old friend. He's got a title, for heaven's sake. He is everything that I am supposed to accomplish in this lifetime. Lady Godalming. I just wish I knew how I felt about it.

MINA - Deep down, you must feel one way or the other about it.

LUCY - I'll tell you my strongest feeling, Mina. It is this. I want to go home. I mean to the house I grew up in, where you and I played. I want that time back. No marriage will accomplish that. Arthur will propose, today or tomorrow, and I will be obliged to marry him. Who knows where he will take me. It cannot be where my heart truly wishes to go.

MINA - Then see to your heart's desire. That is what you have to fight for.

1-9: Inside the Castle

Harker is standing at stage right. Lights low on the rest or the stage.

HARKER - Dearest Mina - My host has treated me with utmost courtesy, and yet, I cannot escape the impression that I am being held a prisoner. By day, I am free to roam those portions of the castle that aren't locked. It is impossible for me to leave this ancient fortress, though even if I could, any attempt to cross this wilderness alone would be madness. By night, I keep company with the Count for a few hours. He tells me stories of ancient wars and bloodshed. When I ask about my seeming captivity, the Count assures me that it is for my own protection. I am prey to a growing fear that I might never see you again, my darling Mina. I cannot sleep, by day or by night. My every waking moment is filled with a profound dread.

As lights come up, Harker sits at a chair, folds the letter and places it into an envelope. Dracula approaches from behind. Harker looks up, sensing his presence before he speaks.

DRACULA - *(looking over his shoulder)* I see, Mr. Harker, that you are diligent in your correspondence with your employer. Also you are faithful in writing to your bride to be.

HARKER - Yes, Count. It is an obligation to the one, and a heartfelt need to the other.

DRACULA - Your loyalty is commendable. You are a most excellent man of affairs, both of the law and of the heart, if I have understood the words correctly.

HARKER - Yes, as usual.

Harker takes a hinged locket from his jacket and opens it. Dracula extends his hand.

DRACULA - Is this the fair Mina to whom so many words are sent?

HARKER - Yes.

DRACULA - *(looking at the picture in the locket)* I see. So beautiful. And with a fire in her eyes. She is a woman with strength of mind and purpose.

HARKER - That's Mina.

DRACULA - You have written to her of the strange old man who lives in the crumbling ruins of his ancestral home.

HARKER - Of course.

DRACULA - *(taking the envelope quickly from Jonathan)* You tell her that I have imprisoned you, that you are a captive, that you have fear for your life.

HARKER - No. I haven't...

DRACULA - *Do not lie to me!* I have read each of your letters. Those to your employer I have sent on their way. Those to your loved one, I have still in my possession.

HARKER - *(rising)* How dare you...

DRACULA - You must not speak now!

HARKER - *(fighting Dracula's gaze)* I will speak when I damn well please. You cannot keep me like this! I don't care what your ways may be, this is not how a civilized man behaves.

DRACULA - *(stepping closer)* The time has come to end our talks of what is civilized. Sit down, Mr. Harker.

HARKER - I will not.

DRACULA - Is it your wish to die?

HARKER - No.

DRACULA - *(capturing his eye)* Good. Then sit down. Take up your pen. You will write to your Mina. I will give you the words. You will have her to think that business has kept you here longer. You must stay just a while, and then she will see you again. But you are well.

HARKER - You can't make me do this...

DRACULA - You will write as I command.

HARKER - No! I will fight you, Dracula!

Dracula takes Harker by the neck, sending the young man into agonizing pain.

DRACULA - Then fight, Jonathan Harker! It will not be your death alone. *(He releases Harker, who collapses into the chair.)* For my family has never killed only a single enemy. Our vengeance must reach the families and loved ones of our enemy as well. I will not stop with your Mina. I will send pain across many generations. So be sure that this is the fight you desire to have.

HARKER - What do you want with me?

DRACULA - *(releasing his gaze on Harker)* Have comfort, young Harker. I have no desire to destroy you. But I will do it if it is your wish.

HARKER - It isn't.

DRACULA - Good. Then take the pen in your hand, and write as I tell you to write.

HARKER - What is to become of me?

DRACULA - Soon, I go on to London, to a new life. But your destiny lies here now.

Lights fade.

1-10: A Garden Walkway at the Westenra Home

————

*A*n *outdoor garden is suggested by light and sounds, center stage. Lucy strolls into view, followed by Arthur Holmwood.*

ARTHUR - Dearest Lucy. At last, I find you in no other company but your own. I desire to speak with you.

LUCY - Yes, Arthur, and I with you.

ARTHUR - Indeed?

LUCY - Yes. I know that you intend to propose to me, perhaps very soon.

ARTHUR - Yes, perhaps.

LUCY - So, I have a question that you must answer honestly.

ARTHUR - What is it?

LUCY - Do you wish to marry me because you love me?

ARTHUR - I am extremely fond of you, Lucy. Well then, yes, I love you.

LUCY - Well, don't. Because I don't love you, Arthur. Not in the way the poets write about.

ARTHUR - I see.

LUCY - Please don't take this the wrong way. I don't love anyone. I never have. I don't think I ever will. I'm not saying I won't marry you. I'm just saying that if you wish to marry me out of love, it would be unfair.

ARTHUR - Then...I don't love you, not in the way the poets mean.

LUCY - Thank God.

ARTHUR - You know, you really are an extraordinary woman, Lucy Westenra. To say a thing like that, it takes character...

LUCY - It is the influence of Mina, you know. She gives me courage.

ARTHUR - So I gather. But courage is honorable. Mina can be impertinent.

LUCY - She is my dearest friend, Arthur. Can you live with that?

ARTHUR - It is to her great credit that you call her your dearest friend. I will honor it.

LUCY - I still don't know if I will accept, Arthur. But then, you haven't actually asked me yet.

ARTHUR - I wasn't going to tonight. I intended to wait until my present business is finished. After that, it can all happen quickly.

LUCY - Then wait. This isn't the time. So, what was it, then, that you had to say to me?

ARTHUR - I suppose I was going to woo you with flowery words. Scratch that. May I walk you through the garden? We can speak of pragmatic and unromantic things.

LUCY - Yes, Arthur. I would enjoy that.

1-11: Dr. Seward's Office

Van Helsing and Seward are presiding over a hypnotic session with Renfield. The subject is seated comfortably in their office, his gaze fixed on the circular swinging pendulum.*

VAN HELSING - Will you please tell us your name?

RENFIELD - Thomas Renfield.

VAN HELSING - Mr. Renfield, do you feel the presence of anyone else, apart from Dr. Seward and myself?

RENFIELD - Yes.

VAN HELSING - Who else is here?

RENFIELD - Mark Stroeb. He's inside my head. He's very quiet right now.

VAN HELSING - Do you think he would agree to talk to us?

RENFIELD - I don't know. It's not up to me.

VAN HELSING - I ask the question of Mark Stroeb himself. Are you here? Can you hear me?

SEWARD - Van Helsing, I don't know that this will...

VAN HELSING - Shhh. Please do not interrupt.

RENFIELD - Is that Dr. Seward?

SEWARD - Yes.

RENFIELD - I remember you. We spent some time together, didn't we?

SEWARD - Mr. Stroeb.

RENFIELD - That's the name I used. Do you know, it isn't my real name at all? It's all mixed up, you see.

VAN HELSING - What of the name Thomas Renfield?

RENFIELD - An invention. Off the top of my head. Just like my story, *The Scarlet Scarab*. Have you read it?

SEWARD - You are an author?

RENFIELD - I've written many books. I'm writing one right now. You're in it, Dr. Seward. And you, Van Helsing. I've put you in my story too. You've given me some excellent ideas during your lecture. Vampires. Charming notion. The blood is the life, Professor.

VAN HELSING - Mr. Renfield insists that it is *you* who are the invention, and that he is the true man.

RENFIELD - It's an evasion, a partial truth. It's not that easy to separate us, you know. I need Thomas Renfield, apprentice bookbinder. Can't have a book without a bookbinder. He does exceptional work.

VAN HELSING - Does it seem strange to you that it is Mr. Renfield who has a job, a wife and family, and that it is you who are hidden in the corners of his mind?

RENFIELD - If only you knew, Professor. But, look for yourself. Try to find this wife and family. Go in search for this bindery that employs him. You will find that they do not exist. He is a skillful liar, our Mr. Renfield. But he is not so wise. He hasn't got the gift of sight. I do. I see things that are, and that are soon to be.

VAN HELSING - That is a common claim among the deluded. How can I know you have such a gift?

RENFIELD - I was hoping you'd ask. There is a disaster at sea, at this very hour. Do you want to hear about it? You'll read it in the papers tomorrow, or the next day. But you may as well get it from me. The trade ship Demeter will be found crashed against the shore, three miles from port. On board they will find only corpses, not a living soul. The captain will be lashed to the ship's helm. His journal will make extraordinary reading.

SEWARD - He's fantasizing.

RENFIELD - We'll see if I am, Dr. Seward. But don't take my word for it. Investigate. That's what you're supposed to do, isn't it? Investigate. I don't know how your story ends just yet, but I'll keep you on alert. I owe it to you.

1-12: The Outdoor Garden at the Westenra Home

The Outdoor Garden again, this time in daylight. Miriam finds Lucy walking. Two adjacent chairs at stage left form a kind of bench.

MIRIAM - *(in an excited whisper)* Lucy, my dear! The moment has come!

LUCY - Mother?

MIRIAM - It is time! Go on. He's waiting to talk to you!

Miriam waves Lucy on with a mischievous grin, then exits. Lucy turns around to find Quincy approaching.

LUCY - Whatever was that about?

QUINCY - I guess that was my doing.

LUCY - Mr Morris.

QUINCY - Call me Quincy. I haven't had much chance to talk to you since the first time I met you.

LUCY - Yes, I suppose.

QUINCY - I'd like to get to know you a little better angel, is all.

LUCY - Thank you. You've been most kind.

QUINCY - I expect most gentlemen are kind to you.

LUCY - Usually.

QUINCY - Well, I guess that's what I wanted to talk about. I've struck up a fine friendship with Lord Godalming. I know he's sort of looking to make you Lady Godalming. I guess you've talked about it.

LUCY - In a preliminary sort of way.

QUINCY - He doesn't seem too optimistic. I guess he figures maybe you don't really love him. This ain't any of my business. I was married once, you see. I have two fine boys, in Texas. Real gentlemen. I loved my wife like I love the stars in the night sky. She passed away two years ago. Cholera. She died young, and that's always hard to abide. But, I've always comforted myself with the thought that I gave her a good home and as much affection as any woman ever had.

LUCY - I'm so sorry. She was lucky to have you.

QUINCY - I hope you won't be upset, but, well... I'm kind of glad you haven't given your assent to his Lordship. I mean, I have the greatest respect for old Holmwood, but I'm about to sort of make myself his rival.

LUCY - I see. Then you are courting me?

QUINCY - Not exactly. I'm not an Englishman. I come from a country where we like to take a more direct approach.

LUCY - How direct?

QUINCY - *(Kneeling before her) This* direct, angel. I'd like to marry you. I know that's sudden and sort of reckless and out of the blue, but I stand by it. I think you're the most beautiful woman I've seen in years. I think I could make you happy. And nothing would please me more than to take you back to my boys and introduce you as my new bride, Lucy Morris. (*He stands back up in awkward silence.*)...Anyway, you're not making a peep, so I've probably made a fool of myself. Won't be the first time...(*He goes to sit on the bench.*)

LUCY - *(following and sitting next to him.)* No, I think it's very sweet. Thank you. It's just that things are so confusing right now.

QUINCY - I know. I kind of launched it on you unexpected.

LUCY - Not really.

QUINCY - No?

LUCY - I'm introduced to a good many men, and a lot of them propose to me. You were a little earlier than most. It does get tiresome.

QUINCY - I see.

LUCY - Oh, I don't mean you, Mr. Morris.

QUINCY - Quincy, please.

LUCY - Quincy. You are perhaps the most charming man who ever asked for my hand.

QUINCY - Okay. That's something.

LUCY - Don't misunderstand, Quincy. I'm not saying no.

QUINCY - You're not?

LUCY - But I'm not saying yes, either. Someone ought to marry you. Maybe that someone should be me. Maybe not. Perhaps when I know you better.

QUINCY - You think so?

LUCY - Can you live with a vague maybe? It's more than I've given to anyone else.

QUINCY - Then I guess I can.

LUCY - So, you've conspired with my mother for this proposal?

QUINCY - Yeah, Miriam encouraged it. I guess she isn't so fond of his Lordship.

LUCY - You know, Mina is right about one thing.

QUINCY - What's that?

LUCY - A woman's mind is made up for her at every step in her life, by every person in her life, and it isn't especially fair.

1-13: Seward's Office

Seward is reading a newspaper. Van Helsing has just arrived.

SEWARD - Have you seen this, Van Helsing?

VAN HELSING - Yes. The wreck of the Demeter.

SEWARD - Every detail is just as he told us.

VAN HELSING - It is perplexing. I can only assume that this is something like sabotage. There was someone on board that ship, someone that Mr. Renfield had knowledge of.

SEWARD - Then you don't credit his claims of precognition?

VAN HELSING - I reserve that explanation as unlikely until there is more proof. But I am troubled. Has it not occurred to you that he seems to have sought us out? His appearance as a volunteer, his cooperation with our treatments. It is as though he wishes to involve himself with us for his own purpose.

SEWARD - I've had the same feeling myself, Professor. What do we do?

VAN HELSING - For now, we continue as before, but carefully. Will you be conducting the session tomorrow?

SEWARD - I've been called to the home of my cousin, Lucy Westenra. She's taken ill.

VAN HELSING - What sort of illness? What are the symptoms.

SEWARD - A general malaise, tiredness, fever, bad dreams. If I didn't know better, I'd say it's owing to anxiety over her engagement. She's just become affianced to Lord Godalming.

1-14: The Lower Rooms of the Castle

———

*H*arker is seen in low light on the upstage platform.

HARKER - For what seemed an eternity, I slept. When I woke, I found myself alone. My door was barred from the other side. I had been left with a small supply of food and water. I heard anguished noises, the sound of a crying infant, high pitched laughter. One night, unexpectedly, I found my prison door open.

A figure is kneeling stage left of Harker. It is a woman bound at the wrists. She beckons from the darkness.

KARENA - *Segitség! Ments meg!* Help me please!

HARKER - Hello. Can you hear me? Is there anyone here?

The lights fully reveal KARENA, a young woman. She kneels on the upper platform, beckoning to Harker. He remains on the lower stage, looking up as if talking through a door.

KARENA - *Ments meg!* Please help

HARKER - Who are you?

KARENA - *Istennek Hála!* Praise God, you are here!

HARKER - *(ascending to platform)* Yes. I'm here. You speak English?

KARENA - Yes. I can speak some. Please to get me out.

HARKER - *(Untying her wrists)* How long have you been imprisoned here?

KARENA - Very long! He is the devil. He has taken my child. My child is dead!

HARKER - It's all right now. You're free. What is your name?

KARENA - Karena. You are my salvation. *Istennek Hála!*

HARKER - Do you know a way out of here?

KARENA - If you will follow me, I know a way.

Two women appear behind Harker and Karena. They are KATJA and ANJA, both lovely, though pale, with alluring, sensuous manners. They are vampire brides of Dracula.

ANJA - I hear a noise.

KATJA - I smell the blood of a stranger.

ANJA - A handsome stranger.

KATJA - Not our master.

ANJA - Such a pity.

HARKER - (*To Karena*) My God, turn around and run. Find the stairs and get to the front door.

ANJA - Please, do not run.

KATJA - We will not hurt you.

ANJA - We like you.

KATJA - Very much.

By now, Karena has stood and joined the other two, her sisters.

ANJA - Karena likes you too. Don't you?

KARENA - He has saved my life.

KATJA - He has saved all our lives, I think.

ANJA - Come closer, Mr. Harker.

She places her hand on his shoulder. Her touch seems to hold Harker in place, although she does not appear to be strong. The other two draw nearer to Harker.

HARKER - No! Oh God, no!

KARENA - There is no danger. These are my sisters. We have looked forward to meeting you. You were promised to us.

HARKER - Where is Count Dracula?

KARENA - He is not here ...

KATJA - For he has risen.

ANJA - He is gone far away. But he has kept his word.

KARENA - Your destiny lies here.

ANJA - Right here.

KATJA - Right here.

The three women surround and overwhelm Harker, whose screams accompany the lights fading out.

1-15: The Parlor at the House of Miriam and Lucy

———

The center of the stage is set with chairs and a side table. Miriam, Lucy and Mina are seated. Lucy wears a silk scarf around her neck. Arthur and Quincy pour and hand out drinks.

ARTHUR - Friends, this night is in honor of my lovely bride-to-be. But first, let me pay my compliments to Miriam. Tonight, you set as rich a table as I have ever enjoyed.

MIRIAM - Thank you, Lord Godalming.*(Turning her attention)* And, may I say what a pleasure it has been to have *you* at our table, Mr. Morris.

QUINCY - Mighty obliged. If nobody minds, I'd like to raise a little toast. To Lord Godalming and his Lady to be. Cheers, my friend. As we say on the prairie, you're one lucky cuss.

ARTHUR - Agreed. To our very bright future, Lucille Westenra.

ALL - *(Except Mina)* Cheers.

MIRIAM - I do worry about Jack. It isn't like him to be this late. I hope nothing has happened.

MINA - Doctor Seward has been wonderful for you, Lucy. You seem much better.

LUCY - I feel fine. And I wouldn't worry so much, mother. He's a very busy man.

MIRIAM - I know, but as *you're* feeling so much better, I thought perhaps he could look after me. I'm on my very last legs.

LUCY - And have been for twenty years.

The guests laugh. There is a jangling of doorbells.

MIRIAM - That could be him.

MINA - (*rising*) I shall be happy to answer, Mrs. Westenra.

Mina exits stage right.

MIRIAM - Thank you, dear. Now, Mr. Morris.

QUINCY - Quincy, please...

MIRIAM - Of course. I must tell you frankly. I am sorry you didn't make a more concerted effort at courting my daughter. You would have made a fine match. I mean no offense to your Lordship, dear Arthur, but your friend here is so ... unpretentious. And I find that refreshing, don't you?

ARTHUR - Er, yes, certainly. One notices that about Quincy right away.

Mina re-enters, followed by Renfield, whose appearance is disheveled

MINA - It's a Mr. Mark Stroeb. He has news of Dr. Seward.

MIRIAM - Is everything all right?

RENFIELD - Oh yes, absolutely! He sent me to tell you that he has encountered some difficulty with his schedule, but he will be joining you within the hour. I would have been here sooner to tell you, only the carriage I rode threw a wheel. As you can see, I am in a state of disarray. By way of introduction, may I present myself to you formally? My name is Thomas Renfield. I am a colleague of Dr. Seward.

MINA - Didn't you tell me at the door that you are Mark Stroeb?

RENFIELD - Did I say that? Oh, I am careless sometimes. That is my pen name, dear lady. I am an author of popular fiction.

LUCY - Have you written anything that I might be familiar with?

RENFIELD - My books may prove shocking to a lady of your fine manners. Perhaps you have heard of them. *Massacre at Scarab Heights, Controversy In Cochineal, The Entomologist's End...*

MIRIAM - So you are an author of murder mysteries?

RENFIELD - Yes! That's correct.

MIRIAM - How delightful! Will you join us for drinks?

Renfield takes the chair formerly occupied by Mina. She stands nearby.

RENFIELD - You are so kind. It is refreshing to see someone so charitable. I was saying only the other day to Mrs. Renfield, that's my wife, that it is rare to find persons of grace in this age. Persons who do not make judgments, persons who look for the real you behind the clothes you wear and the manners you possess. It gives me hope.

MINA - Did you say you are a colleague of Dr. Seward?

RENFIELD - He and I are engaged in serious work on the psychology of the displaced mind.

MINA - And you are an author of fiction.

RENFIELD - I am many things. When the doctor arrives, I do not doubt that he will see Miss Lucy through her ailments. He is a most excellent practitioner. I am not simply a colleague, you see. I have, on more than one occasion, been his patient as well.

As his speech continues, Renfield removes from his coat, first, a dainty tea plate, then, a small sack tied with a ribbon.

RENFIELD - Now Mrs. Westenra, I foresee a satisfactory end to your medical complaints also. I have the gift of foresight, you see. It is this talent that has aroused such active interest from Dr. Seward. As to you, Miss Murray, do not give another thought to your Jonathan. He is well looked after, and will call for you presently. Yes, I am nearly certain of that. Oh, I know my precognitive gifts do astonish. By the way, I hope you will not take offense if I eat my own supper at this time. I'm on a strict diet, and carry my own food with me. Doctor's orders, you know. The blood is most happily the life.

Renfield opens the small sack, and sprinkles a generous number of insects onto the small plate. He begins to eat these as happily as one might eat a plate of biscuits. By now, Lucy and Miriam have left their chairs. Astonished reactions give way to panic.

ARTHUR - That man is insane!

MIRIAM - Will you leave this place at once!

RENFIELD - Oh, if only I could. This is awfully embarrassing.

Arthur approaches Renfield, who climbs up onto the chair, defensively, as one might react to a mouse.

ARTHUR - You heard the lady. You are not welcome here. I insist you leave!

LUCY - Good lord, Mina.

MINA - Just stay calm, Lucy. I don't think he's dangerous.

RENFIELD - Not dangerous, no! You see? She understands.

QUINCY - Listen, Mister. You've been asked, and you've been told. I'll be happy to drag you out of here if I have to.

Renfield leaps from the chair and takes Quincy by surprise, twisting Quincy's arm behind his back.

RENFIELD - You mean by force? Sorry, but I don't have much respect for classless people who must resort to *brute strength!*

Holmwood manages to force Renfield off of Quincy. He takes Renfield by the collar.

ARTHUR - I have every right to kill you right here!

Renfield strikes a blow to Holmwood, then pounces on top of him.

RENFIELD - You haven't and you know it. You and I answer to a higher power! On the other hand, I will be shown mercy, for I know not what I do. I'm going to enjoy causing you harm, Lord Godalming.

Mina has picked up a metal pitcher and now swings it down and strikes Renfield a blow on the back of the head. Renfield is stunned, then falls unconscious. Mina gives Arthur a smug look.

MINA - I don't know how you'll ever thank me.

Lucy falls into a heap on the floor.

MIRIAM - Mina! Lucy's fainted!

Another clatter of doorbells.

MINA - Would you answer that, Quincy? Lucy, Lucy, everything is all right.

Quincy leaves to answer the door. Arthur stands and regains his composure.

MIRIAM - Mina, what is happening? Everything has gone completely out of control. I can't stand it!

MINA - Don't worry, Miriam. Everything will be fine.

Dr. Seward and Professor Van Helsing enter, followed by Quincy.

SEWARD - What's happened?

MINA - We had a surprise visitor. A friend of yours, I think.

VAN HELSING - Renfield!

SEWARD - I'll attend to him, Van Helsing. Will you please look after Lucy?

MIRIAM - Yes, please help my Lucy, and someone get this creature out of my house!

ARTHUR - I'll go and find a constable.

Seward draws a syringe from his bag and kneels next to Renfield.

SEWARD - I'm sedating him in case he comes around. I shall have my wardens come and retrieve him.

QUINCY - He's pretty strong. I think he was about to give His Lordship a good whomping.

ARTHUR - Miss Murray. It looks as though I owe you a debt.

MINA - It needed to be done. I am not your enemy, Arthur.

VAN HELSING - The girl is awake, Dr. Seward. *(To Lucy)* Hello, young Miss, I am Professor Van Helsing. Everything is all right.

He immediately removes the scarf and begins to examine her face and neck. Lucy tries to prevent him from doing so.

LUCY - I'm fine. Forgive me. I was overwhelmed.

VAN HELSING - Don't be afraid, my dear. I must only have one glance. *(He looks behind the scarf, then gently puts it back)*

MIRIAM - Is she all right?

LUCY - I'm fine, mother.

VAN HELSING - I would suggest that you take your daughter to her room. Let her rest a while. Then I would speak with you.

They all rise. Mina takes Lucy's arm. Miriam, Quincy and Holmwood follow as Lucy is led out of the room.

MIRIAM - Let's have you lie down for a while.

MINA - I've got you, Lucy.

All are gone except for Seward, Van Helsing and the unconscious Renfield.

VAN HELSING - My guess is that Renfield took your journal, Dr. Seward.

SEWARD - I will never forgive myself for being so careless. I never thought he would intrude on my family.

VAN HELSING - There is a far more serious concern. We have our vampire, Jack. The marks on the young lady's throat are unmistakable.

SEWARD - Forgive me, Professor. This is hard to accept.

VAN HELSING - I know, my friend. It is hard to tell you. My suspicions about Renfield are correct. There is some link between him and this vampire. It is not coincidence that the curse falls on your loved ones.

SEWARD - (*searching Renfield's coat pockets for the journal*) Indeed. My journal holds much information on Lucy. And here it is.

VAN HELSING - I should see this journal, Dr. Seward.

SEWARD - (*putting it in his pocket*) No, Professor, that isn't possible.

VAN HELSING - Why not?

SEWARD - It is a personal document, not a medical record.

VAN HELSING - So be it. But if we are to help Miss Lucy, I think it is important that we have no secrets from one another.

SEWARD - We have none, Van Helsing. None that matter.

1-16: Lucy's Boudoir

The box on the upstage platform is turned short side out and draped to look like an elegant bed. Two chairs with small side table are placed stage right of the bed. Mina steps forward.

MINA - June 29th. My worries about Lucy only increase. For three days, I have watched as she seems to recover, only to awaken the next day in worse condition than before. Van Helsing has ordered the strangest treatments for her. Blood transfusions, and a vigil to be kept every night. Arthur Holmwood and Quincy Morris have taken on that responsibility. In the face of all of this, Lucy has shown tremendous courage. My heart nearly breaks at the thought that she could lose this fight. *(She exits)*

Lucy and Arthur are seated in the chairs. A transfusion has just taken place. Van Helsing is attending to the apparatus on the table.

ARTHUR - I don't understand, Van Helsing. We've been supplying her with fresh blood for two days, and she continues to lose more. Where is all that blood going?

VAN HELSING - It is a rare condition, Lord Godalming, a degenerative disease of the blood cells. But this treatment has been found to work. I require your patience.

ARTHUR - I suppose you have it. How are you feeling, Lucy?

LUCY - Better. You have good blood, Lord Godalming. Our children will be pillars of strength.

Van Helsing applies bandages as he removes the needles, first from Arthur, and then from Lucy.

VAN HELSING - And we are done. Now, just hold that, Lord Godalming. Lucy, press down on this while I prepare the bandage.

LUCY - Bless you, Arthur, for doing this.

ARTHUR - My last drop, if necessary, is yours.

VAN HELSING - If you will come with me, Godalming, I would like to wash that spot before I bandage it.

ARTHUR - Certainly. I'll be back, Lucy.

LUCY - Could you bring Mina?

ARTHUR - Yes. Of course.

(Arthur and Van Helsing exit. Seward is alone with Lucy)

SEWARD - I'm glad you're feeling better.

LUCY - The truth is, I'm not. Last night, I thought the worst had passed. I went to bed full of blood and courage. And then came those horrible dreams again. I woke up sick and frail. Oh God, Jack, I'm so frightened...

Seward goes to Lucy's side and takes her in his arms.

SEWARD - Please don't cry, Lucy. We're all here to get you through this. But you must continue to be brave.

LUCY - You are the brave one, Jack. This has to be awful for you.

SEWARD - What else could I expect? You had to marry someday, and it was never going to be me. He's a good man. He will take excellent care of you. (*He kisses her gently on the lips.*) My God, Lucy, I love you so much. It doesn't matter that I can never be with you, as long as you're happy. But you have got to live. If I lose you to this sickness, it will kill me.

LUCY - Yes, it will kill me too. (*There is a pause*) That's a joke.

SEWARD - Yes. I see.

LUCY - That's got to be a good sign, if I can make a joke, I mean.

Seward rises.

SEWARD - Yes, it's a good sign.

LUCY - You are the only man I have ever loved. I will always feel this way, never forget that. And this is the last time I will ever say it. Please, Jack, promise me that you will never speak of it again.

SEWARD - I cannot promise, but I will try.

Enter Miriam, followed by Mina.

MIRIAM - Hello, Jack.

SEWARD - Miriam.

MIRIAM - What luck to have you in our family. Lucy, do you mind if I share your bed tonight? If I'm going to worry about you, I may as well stay by your side.

SEWARD - I think it's an excellent idea, Miriam.

LUCY - You may sleep my side tomorrow night, Mina.

MINA - Yes, Lucy. That would be fine. I must be going for tonight. I'll be back first thing in the morning.

Lucy goes to Mina and takes her hand. She leads Mina to take one step off of the platform, isolating the two of them for a moment.

LUCY - *(quietly)* Mina. Promise me something.

MINA - Of course.

LUCY - Promise you won't hate me for the decision I've made.

MINA - Lucy! You must never think that!

LUCY - It's something I had to do. I can't explain it.

MINA - You will never need to.

MIRIAM - *(calling over to them)* Lucy, come now. You can talk to Mina tomorrow.

LUCY - Yes, Mother.

Lucy and Mina step back up to the platform and Lucy sits along the side of the bed, while Miriam goes to the opposite side.

MIRIAM - Mina, thank you for being such a dear.

MINA - Of course. Good night, Mrs. Westenra. And good night to you, Lucy.

LUCY - Will you pray for me? I don't suppose you believe in that sort of thing.

MINA - If it will help you, yes. I will.

LUCY - There is a soul, Mina. You must never doubt that.

MINA - For your sake, Lucy, I do believe it.

She kisses Lucy on the forehead and exits. Arthur and Van Helsing enter the room just as she leaves. Van Helsing gathers the transfusion apparatus into a doctor's bag.

ARTHUR - Good night, my dear. I just wanted you to know, Quincy and I will be outside your door all night. If you wake, if you feel frightened, if you need anything, we will be here.

LUCY - Thank you, Arthur. Good night.

ARTHUR - Good night, Lucy.

Arthur and Quincy take position downstage, just beneath the platform, as though standing guard to the room. Van Helsing passes by the two of them, nods his approval of their vigil, and exits. The lights go down.

From the darkened silence, Miriam sits upright in the bed. As she speaks, she does not see that both Arthur and Quincy have entered the room.

MIRIAM - Lucy, are you awake? I'm having such trouble sleeping. I'll be back, my dear.

Miriam rises from the bed and steps away. Quincy grabs her from behind and holds a cloth over her face. She struggles for a brief time, but soon collapses. Arthur and Quincy drag her a few feet away, to a place just behind the chairs.

The two men set a small tray between them on the ground. Quincy lights a candle and places it on the tray. Arthur takes a small bit of incense and sets it aflame. The two begin to chant slowly.

ARTHUR & QUINCY -

Ave Satanas, filium draconis citamus

Ave Satanas, filium draconis citamus

Dracula vocamus, Dracula vocamus

The last line of this chant is repeated until Dracula appears behind them. They cease chanting and turn to bow to him. He takes Quincy's face in his hands and regards the man for a moment. Then he nods toward Arthur. He makes a gesture and the two men extinguish the candle and return to their position outside the room.

Dracula goes to the bed. He uncovers Lucy and gently takes her head into his hands. He strokes her neck, then bends his face down to it. As he bites, Lucy's eyes open wide, her face frozen in silent terror. Lights fade.

End Act One

Act Two

During the interval, the box is placed long side out on the upstage platform. Lucy lies on top, arms crossed and holding a funereal bouquet. She is draped with a white veil-like shroud. She remains motionless throughout the remainder of the interval. Shadows of tombstones are seen against the backdrop. The sounds are quiet and unsettling, the mood somber. Silence returns before the second act begins.

2 -1: A Graveyard By Day

Lights up, amid sounds of birdsong conveying that it is now daytime. Mina stands on the stage alone and speaks.

MINA - Dear Jonathan. I continue to write, though I begin to wonder if you will ever read these words. I have received only one reply, and that has failed to reassure me of your wellbeing. Lucy and Miriam have been laid to rest in a family vault. Lucy's cousin, Dr. Jack Seward, is in the hold of severe grief, I do not know how he continues his practice. Perhaps he does not.

Mina crosses over to Jack Seward, seated on the platform at stage right.

MINA - I thought you might be here, Jack.

SEWARD - Yes.

MINA - Perhaps you ought to get away. Out of London, I mean. For a while.

SEWARD - I have responsibilities, Miss Murray.

MINA - Responsibilities you are in no condition to attend to. Van Helsing has suggested that he be put in charge for...

SEWARD - No, Mina! Do not heed him! He is a madman.

MINA - What are you talking about?

SEWARD - This is all his fault. His treatments, his delusions about vampires...

MINA - Vampires?

SEWARD - Oh yes. He didn't tell you about that, now, did he! That was his rare blood condition. Vampires. And I bought into this lie, Mina. Do you want to know what he intended to do to poor Lucy? He wanted to cut off her head. But only after he had impaled her on a pointed stake ...

Seward is crazed with grief. Mina embraces him.

MINA - Jack, get away from this place, do whatever it takes.

SEWARD - Lucy adored you.

MINA - She loved you as well.

SEWARD - *(breaking away)* I'm lost. I'm... I'm afraid.

MINA - We're all suffering, Jack.

SEWARD - I know...

Enter Van Helsing

VAN HELSING - Dr. Seward.

SEWARD - I have nothing to say to you, Professor.

VAN HELSING - It is Miss Murray I wish to speak to.

SEWARD - Are you going to feed her the same poison you've given me? I wish Professor Arminius could be here to share in this new knowledge. I'm sure he would be proud to find his protege engaged in the work of ghouls.

VAN HELSING - I am sorry if I have given offense. I must speak what I feel is the truth.

SEWARD - *(rising)* Then go ahead, Van Helsing. Tell Mina what you told me. Don't change a word of it. Tell her how you wish to desecrate Lucy's body. Tell it to her now, so she will see you for what you really are. Miss Murray, I leave you to this man I once admired. I beg you to listen with a rational mind. Good bye, Mina.

Seward exits

VAN HELSING - In ordinary circumstances, he is right to think me crazy.

MINA - If what he tells me is true, Van Helsing, anyone would think so.

VAN HELSING - This is so, Miss Murray. I had hoped to prove to him that my words are true, though hard to believe. But he is consumed with grief. You have kept your head. I wish to share with you all that I know of this case.

MINA - Professor, do you truly intend to butcher my departed friend?

VAN HELSING - No one could perform such an atrocious act, not unless they knew for certain that it was necessary. I wish there was some way I could spare you the pain. Some way I could prevent the shock of seeing a loved one return from the grave. You have my promise that I will not make a single move unless you have approved of it. You will decide, based on what you see.

MINA - What could possibly have brought you to such extraordinary views?

VAN HELSING - I had a daughter. Her name was Sara. She fell prey to the same sickness that Miss Lucy suffered. Of course, I did not believe when I was told. I had to see for myself. And I had to watch her die twice. It was Professor Arminius who drove the stake into her heart. And I hated him for it. But I had seen her rise, had felt how cold and dead was her skin, how the scent of corruption and death was upon her. She is at rest now.

MINA - I'm sorry.

VAN HELSING - Yes, well, that was many years ago. I have since been consumed with the search for these vampires. All of my science I have put to this end. But there is a limit to what science can tell me, and I no longer have the faith I once had.

MINA - How do you mean?

VAN HELSING - I once believed in a merciful God. But I cannot now see how this could be. And I cannot accept that the soul of my beautiful daughter must be consumed in the fires of Hell. So I have abandoned my belief in such things.

MINA - As have I.

VAN HELSING - The enemy we face is powerful. Sometimes, he is controlling many people, making them to do his bidding. I have now much evidence to suspect that the patient Thomas Renfield is himself a servant of the vampire, Voivode Dracul.

MINA - I'm sorry, Professor, what was that name?

VAN HELSING - Dracul. He is the most powerful of the vampires.

MINA - Would that name be in any way related to a Count Dracula?

VAN HELSING - Yes. They are the same.

MINA - My fiance, Jonathan Harker, is in Transylvania now in the company of a nobleman named Dracula.

VAN HELSING - What did you say?

MINA - My fiance, Jonathan. His client is a Count Dracula.

VAN HELSING - You are certain that this is his name?

MINA - Yes.

VAN HELSING - Then Mr. Harker is in serious danger. I suspect that the vampire is already in London, that he fed on Miss Lucy and took her from us. I fear for your fiance if he remained behind. He may well be a prisoner.

MINA - It's clear that you are serious, but I am not prepared to believe that this is what happened to Lucy. As for Jonathan, I will ask after him, Van Helsing. And when the whole truth of this matter is known, I will not hesitate to reveal you.

VAN HELSING - Let it be so. I pray I am wrong, Miss Murray.

She exits. Van Helsing slowly follows after her. On the other end of the stage, Quincy enters with Seward

SEWARD - What brings you here, Mr. Morris?

QUINCY - That priest Lucy and Miriam were friends with. His church is around here?

SEWARD - It is quite close by.

QUINCY - I wish you'd help me find him. I got somethin' in the way of a confession, I guess. I want you to know about it.

SEWARD - I can't imagine what you mean.

QUINCY - It's about Miss Lucy.

SEWARD - Then I insist on knowing.

QUINCY - Come on, then. But it ain't gonna make you happy.

They exit.

2-2: A Church Graveyard at Night

The setting remains the same. The lights lower, and the sounds of night begin to play.

Lucy pulls back the veil that covers her and sits up on her funeral bier. She stands and steps onto the lower stage, then exits as bells toll quietly in the distance. She is beautiful, but pale.

Two seats representing a bench are placed at Stage Left. A young boy, SIMON, is walking in the cold night. He stops for a moment, puts down his lantern, and hugs himself, trying to stay warm. A young girl, HARRIET, dressed in a nightgown, appears across the way. She sings an eerie melody.

HARRIET *(singing)*

Speak no whispers in the night, don't make a sound

Close your eyes 'til morning light touches the ground

Children who fear and children who weep

Let the shadows of the night enter their sleep

SIMON - Harriet? Harriet!

Harriet crosses slowly to him.

HARRIET - Hello, Simon.

SIMON - What are you doing here? I could never get you to come into the graveyard before, not even on a dare.

HARRIET - It doesn't frighten you, does it?

SIMON - 'Course not!

HARRIET - I'm so glad you came to find me, Simon. I was afraid you wouldn't be able to get away.

SIMON - You're causing an awful fuss, running out like this. There was coppers and everything, asking me questions like they knew I was on to you.

HARRIET - Did you keep my secret, Simon? You'd better have kept it.

SIMON - 'Course I did. So are you coming home or not?

HARRIET - No, Simon. I can't. I know of somewhere better than home. I want to show you.

SIMON - Harriet, please come back. Mum's so worried.

HARRIET - *(taking his hands)* Don't be stupid, Simon. Come here. *(tugging at him)* Come here, Simon, it's all right.

SIMON - Your hands are cold.

HARRIET - There's someone I want you to meet.

She begins leading him toward the bench.

SIMON - I don't know.

HARRIET - Oh really, Simon. Don't act like a baby. There's nothing to be afraid of.

Lucy appears, almost ghostly, but lovely.

HARRIET - Oh, look Simon. It's her.

SIMON - Who is she?

HARRIET - She's my friend. Isn't she beautiful?

SIMON - I don't like this.

HARRIET - Come on, Simon. She's nice.

LUCY - It's all right, Harriet. Remember, you were afraid of me once.

HARRIET - This is my brother Simon. He's been very good. He's kept our secret.

LUCY - What a clever boy. Do you like chocolates, Simon?

HARRIET - Go on, Simon. Talk to 'er. It's all right.

LUCY - You do like chocolates, don't you?

SIMON - Yes, Mum.

LUCY - How lucky. I have some right here. Won't you share them with me?

SIMON - Yes'm. Thank you, Mum.

Lucy leads Simon to the bench, where she sits, inviting him to join her.

LUCY - Please, call me Lucy. Here. Aren't they pretty, all wrapped up like that? Go ahead, it's all right.

Simon sits on the bench, at some distance, as he unwraps and eats a chocolate.

LUCY - It's a shame to have to unwrap such a lovely thing, isn't it? You have to destroy such a shiny bauble just to get to the sweets inside. *(Harriet giggles)* Don't laugh, Harriet. He'll get over his fear, just as you did. Come closer, Simon.

SIMON - I'd rather not.

LUCY - Don't you like me? I like you, Simon, very much.

HARRIET - Go on, Simon. Don't be mean.

LUCY - That's it, Simon. Come closer. I've got more chocolates to give you.

She gently touches him.

SIMON - You're cold, too.

LUCY - Yes, Simon, but we will soon be warm. Have another chocolate. They're sweet, just like you.

She strokes his hair as he continues to eat. She begins to hum the lullaby that Harriet was singing earlier. Simon's gaze finally meets hers. She lowers his head onto her lap and exposes his neck. Harriet laughs slowly as the lights fade.

2-3: The Office of Holloman and Walker, Solicitors

———

A single chair is placed up left. Renfield sits on it, holding a large bound ledger. He is looking through it. He is more professionally dressed than we have yet seen him. We hear the jingle of the bell over a door. As Mina enters, he keeps his body angled away from her, as if too busy in his books to look at her. She does not at first recognize him.

MINA - Excuse me. I need information.

RENFIELD - We all do, dear lady. I am not in the business of providing it.

MINA - I came to inquire about Jonathan Harker.

RENFIELD - This is the office of Walker and Holloman, realtors. Are you sure you are in the right place?

MINA - I am certain. May I speak to Mr. Walker, or Mr. Holloman?

RENFIELD - I cannot possibly allow you to see Mr. Holloman, as he is dead.

MINA - Are you trying to vex me?

RENFIELD - *(turning to face her)* Never. I speak in earnest.

MINA - You!

RENFIELD - Eukariah Walker at your service.

MINA - What is the meaning of this, Mr. Renfield?

RENFIELD - I wish I had an answer for that. I haven't. This is awkward, dear lady...

MINA - You aren't really Mr. Walker.

RENFIELD - Oh, but I am, you see. It is only a matter of coincidence that I also happen to be Mark Stroeb, noted author. As to Thomas Renfield, I'm afraid he's mostly a dream anymore.

MINA - Jonathan Harker. What do you know of him?

RENFIELD - Harker? Oh, a great deal. Quite a promising young man. He's away right now, but then, you knew that.

MINA - *(increasingly befuddled)* This isn't a game, Mr Ren ... oh!

RENFIELD - But of course, you must be worried. And who can blame you? I mean, he wasn't supposed to be gone so long. And then there are those letters he sends. *(brandishing an envelope from the ledger)* There's something odd about them. I mean, the style, the choice of words. Compare this note we got last week to the one we received a month ago, and it's almost like he's a different person.

MINA - I am warning you. I will take this outrageous affair to the highest authorities.

RENFIELD - But, my dear, he's fine. He says so right here. Why, even Count Dracula gives an excellent report of him.

MINA - You have communications from the Count?

Arthur Holmwood has entered the room.

ARTHUR - We have spoken to him face to face, Miss Murray.

MINA - Arthur, what are you doing here?

ARTHUR - Protecting my interests. *(aside to her)* I don't know if it has occurred to you, but you and I are the only sane persons in this room.

MINA - Then I rely on your help.

ARTHUR - Oh, you shall have it. Count Dracula is already a resident of our fair city, Miss Murray. He's been here for some time. Jonathan, well, let us say he elected to stay in Transylvania. He's unearthed some compelling opportunities.

MINA - My God, Arthur, what would *you* know about it?

ARTHUR - Everything, my dear. It's no coincidence that you find me here. In the company I keep, there are no coincidences. You and I are involved in a plan. We are part of something far more important than our own petty lives.

MINA - Arthur, I beg of you, for the sake of Lucy whom we both loved, tell me what all this means.

ARTHUR - Ah yes, dear departed Lucy. Her memory is our bond. I guess the wedding is off now, just as you wanted. It wasn't my decision. It was his, the Master. I would have enjoyed spending some time with her. Charming girl.

MINA - Please tell me you didn't murder her...

ARTHUR - Of course not. I wouldn't dream of it. She was chosen, Mina. That's all there is to it. He is a great man, the Count. We call him Nosferatu. He has conquered empires. With our help, he will do it again. You are part of a great moment, a small part, but you should be grateful.

MINA - No. Oh, dear God...

ARTHUR - I'm so sorry. But in the long run, it doesn't matter much, these little sacrifices we make. Lucy could never have accomplished anything on her own as important as what she has done for us now. As for Miriam, well, that was regrettable, but just an accident. We only applied some chloroform. Her heart did the rest. But she was unhappy anyway. If you ask me, we did the old girl a favor...

Enraged, Mina charges at Arthur.

MINA - I swear I'll kill you!

Arthur calmly draws a pistol and extends it toward Mina.

ARTHUR - You're very impressive, my dear.

Renfield stands behind Mina with the ledger. He delivers a blow to the back of her head, much in the same manner that Mina knocked him out previously. Mina staggers, dazed, before collapsing with a groan.

RENFIELD - Now, that *is* satisfying.

ARTHUR - Thank you, Mr. Renfield. I will tell our Master of your progress. He will be pleased.

RENFIELD - It's a pity. She's very lovely. I tried to warn her.

2-4: The Catacombs Beneath Carfax Abbey

Note: This will be the setting for all remaining scenes until the Epilogue. The box on the upper platform is brought to its edge, suggesting a kind of altar. Other areas of the stage are lit as the action moves from one sequence to another. Characters quickly appear and disappear either into the wings, or behind black pipe and drape.

Shadows and sound suggest a cold, wet, dripping catacombs. Shadow images include cracked pillars, destroyed crosses, broken doors and mysterious passageways.

2-4A: The Lower Catacombs

Seward and Shaugnessy have entered the catacombs. Seward carries a lantern. Shaugnessy has a small satchel in which is kept a vial of holy water, along with two daggers. He also carries a wooden stake, long and sharp.

SHAUGNESSY - I need to stop a moment. *(He drops the large stake)* I don't like it. It's heavy. And I tremble to think we might actually need to use it.

SEWARD - Leave it here, then. We have pistols.

SHAUGNESSY - That won't kill them, not according to your notes.

SEWARD - They aren't *my* notes.

SHAUGNESSY - *(reaching into his satchel)* Perhaps this weapon will be more effective.

SEWARD - What is it?

SHAUGNESSY - A consecrated dagger doused in holy water.

SEWARD - Do you really think we will find vampires here?

SHAUGNESSY - My real hope is that this will end up being a merry prank, perpetrated by some bored wealthy friends. That is my hope.

SEWARD - I have an unshakable feeling we are entering a trap, Father.

SHAUGNESSY - I have that feeling too. But what else could we have done?

SEWARD - We could have called the police.

SHAUGNESSY - To help us break in here? It's bad enough they almost caught us opening Miss Lucy's crypt.

Lucy appears in a passageway

SEWARD - Dear God.

LUCY - Jack? Did you come looking for me, Jack?

SEWARD - You're not real …

LUCY - Are you surprised to see me?

SEWARD - Lucy...

SHAUGNESSY - She was dead, Jack. I know that she was dead.

LUCY - No, Father Shaugnessy. I was only sleeping. You put me into the tomb while I was asleep. Jack, come to me. Aren't you happy to see me?

SEWARD - If you were really Lucy...

LUCY - But I am. Jack, don't be afraid of me. I love you. We can be together now. Forever. It's what we've always wanted.

Shaugnessy sprinkles holy water toward Lucy. She cries out as though she has been stung.

LUCY - Get that away from me.

SHAUGNESSY - It is only holy water, my dear. It cannot hurt you.

Lucy goes to Seward and beckons to him.

LUCY - Jack, tell him to leave us alone. He wants to hurt me. There's nothing wrong with me, Jack.

SEWARD - My God, Father Shaugnessy, how can we be sure?

SHAUGNESSY - In the name of the Father, and of the Son, and of the Holy Spirit...

Lucy screams as the water touches her. She grabs Seward into an embrace.

LUCY - Make him stop, Jack!

SHAUGNESSY - Get away from her, Jack.

SEWARD - Damn you for being right, Van Helsing.

Seward draws his knife, unseen by Lucy.

SHAUGNESSY - Do it, Jack.

LUCY - You are so warm, my love. Don't be afraid, Jack.

SEWARD - I will go mad. I know it.

He stabs Lucy. Her cry echoes through the catacombs. The children, Harriet and Simon, appear from behind. They join in the screaming. Harriet attacks Father Shaugnessy, Simon runs to Seward. Shaugnessy draws his pistol.

SHAUGNESSY - God forgive me.

The lights BLACKOUT as one GUNSHOT is heard, followed by a child's scream, then another shot.

2-4B: The Altar Chamber

———

Mina lies on the altar. She is asleep. Renfield makes his way to her, and looks at her tenderly. She opens her eyes and stirs a little. She is weak and not too coherent.

RENFIELD - Are you awake?

MINA - Help me...

RENFIELD - Oh, I have been, dear lady, I have been. So many things to arrange. It will be over soon. You're going on a voyage. You are to be reunited with your Jonathan.

MINA - Jonathan...

RENFIELD - Yes, just as I foresaw. The master's decision. You are going to play a key role in the plan. And you will be rewarded, just as I am given all the lives I can eat in exchange for my services. I see a bright future for you and your Jonathan. The Order of the Reckoning. We are all part of it. This is a great time. Everything is about to go up in flames. We'll be lighting the torch. And out of the ashes, a great new civilization will rise, free from death itself. That is the great vision. I am pleased to have arranged so many parts of it.

Renfield lifts Mina to a sitting position and smooths her hair.

RENFIELD - You must make yourself presentable now. You will soon meet our Master. It is an exceptional honor. I can't wait to see how things work themselves out. I never know how my novels will end until I've written the last word.

MINA - Get me out of here. Will you please help me, for God's sake!

RENFIELD - In good time. I have to go now. You are a valiant heroine.

Renfield leaves. A shadowy figure approaches. Mina strains to see in the darkness. The figure speaks. It seems to be Jonathan Harker.

HARKER - Mina. Wake up!

MINA - Jonathan?

HARKER - Yes, Mina.

MINA - Thank God! Jonathan, come closer...

She tries to walk, but falters.

HARKER -

Do not try to approach me now, Mina.

MINA - Get me out of here, Jonathan...

HARKER - I can't help you. We will be together again soon.

MINA - What is going on?

HARKER - You are beneath Carfax Abbey. It is the property I secured for the Count. You are his guest.

MINA - There is something terrible going on here. We've got to get away.

HARKER - Not yet, Mina. I am not really here. I am a shadow.

MINA - What are you talking about?

HARKER - I am as insubstantial as a dream. I cannot touch you.

Dracula appears directly behind Mina. He appears stronger now, his face almost wolf-like and fierce, his hair now black instead of gray. From behind Mina he wraps his arms around her. He speaks the next few lines simultaneously with Harker. Mina's vision has been a trick of the mind played on her by the vampire.

HARKER/ DRACULA - *(together)* But you may feel the touch of another hand. Sleep now, Mina.

MINA - Jonathan...

The lights fade on Jonathan. The vision of Harker is gone.

DRACULA - You will see your Jonathan again. Sleep now.

Dracula leads Mina back to the altar, and upon placing her there, prepares to bite her throat. The lights fade as Mina screams.

2-4C: A Catacombs Passageway Nearby

Van Helsing appears with a black bag and a lantern. He is alone. He hears Mina's cry.

VAN HELSING - Miss Murray, is that you? *(Another yell from Mina)* It is all right, Miss Murray. I have come to help.

Quincy appears from Stage Left. He is armed with a gun.

QUINCY - Get away from here, old man.

VAN HELSING - Mr. Morris. Jack said I would find you here.

QUINCY - You'd better go away. I have orders to shoot anyone who tries to pass by.

VAN HELSING - I have come at the request of Dr. Seward, because of what you told him.

QUINCY - I'm sorry, Professor. He wasn't meant to share that with anyone else.

MINA - *(From the altar, in darkness)* Help me!

VAN HELSING - That is Miss Murray! I must go to her...

Van Helsing begins to hurry past Quincy, who fires his gun. Van Helsing is hit in the right shoulder. He falls to the ground.

QUINCY - Sorry about that, old man. It was my head if I let you go any further.

Renfield appears, agitated by the noise, and shocked when he sees what has transpired.

RENFIELD - No! Are you out of your mind? I was to bring this man to the master alive!

QUINCY - I didn't know you were bringing him here at all.

RENFIELD - *(kneeling by Van Helsing)* Of course, you imbecile! It's all right. You've wounded him, but I don't think it's fatal. That's very lucky for you.

QUINCY - I'm sorry. I just got a little over-excited. It's not my fault that he wouldn't listen.

RENFIELD - Why don't you go back to your post now? You're in enough trouble, I don't want to know what would happen if you were to make another mistake.

QUINCY - Hey, I don't suppose maybe you could not mention who did this?

RENFIELD - There's no keeping anything from him.

Quincy exits, Renfield assists Van Helsing through one of the passages.

2-4D: The Altar Chamber

Mina is asleep on the altar, facing away from the audience. Van Helsing is propped against the stage left side of the altar. Dracula enters and sits atop the altar, looking down on him. Van Helsing is visibly in pain, his arm and shoulder wrapped in a makeshift sling. There is blood on his clothing.

DRACULA - Abraham Van Helsing. You were bleeding. I have seen to your wounds. I trust you will recover.

VAN HELSING - Dracula?

DRACULA - As you would call me. I am to understand that you have declared yourself my nemesis.

VAN HELSING - You killed my daughter.

DRACULA - I gave her new life. It was your own colleague who destroyed her. You know that.

VAN HELSING - I have sworn to kill you.

DRACULA - Yes. This is why I have brought you here. I won't stop you.

VAN HELSING - What do you want with me?

DRACULA - Nothing. I owe you this courtesy. You have done me a great honor, telling your people of my power and existence.

VAN HELSING - No one believes me.

DRACULA - That is the way of your modern world. But we are wasting time. You must have things you want to ask of me. So many questions a man of science would want to know. This is your only chance. I will not grant this audience again.

VAN HELSING - So you are going to answer my questions and that is all.

DRACULA - That is all. Come now, Professor. What is it you really want to know? I have the answer. Think about it. I am a man who has died, who has felt his heart stop beating and his blood stop flowing. I have been dead, Van Helsing, and have returned to life. Surely there are questions that only I can answer for you.

VAN HELSING - My daughter...

DRACULA - Was her soul confined to the fires of Hell? That is what you want to know, isn't it. And the answer is this. Her soul does not burn. And it is because there is no such thing. No soul, no eternal light, no eternal damnation. So now you know. The only immortality is that which I have found. It is a gift that I now offer to you, Professor. Everlasting life as a creature of the night.

VAN HELSING - Is that really any kind of life?

DRACULA - Do you dare to find out for yourself?

VAN HELSING - No. I would rather you killed me.

DRACULA - I have no desire to do this. I want to share with you the chance to know - know everything. You could continue your work, but with new knowledge and new power.

VAN HELSING - Why don't I believe you, Dracul, son of the dragon?

Dracula picks up Van Helsing's bag and opens it. He withdraws a wooden cross and a dagger.

DRACULA - Because it is your profession to doubt. And yet, what do I find among your weapons of war? You take the precautions of a frightened peasant. Here, take it. I am not going to harm you. *(Hands belongings back to Van Helsing)* Go ahead. You have the advantage. One thrust and you have won. *Well, go on!* Take your victory!

VAN HELSING - You will not let me.

DRACULA - On the contrary, Professor. I will do nothing. I am tired, Van Helsing. I came to this city to bring about a new empire. But I no longer have the will to carry out so great a conquest. I wish to rest.

VAN HELSING - Then take your own life.

DRACULA - My instincts will not allow it. The vampire nature fights my will. They are two different things, you know. The vampire wishes to go on, the old man inside of the vampire is ready to die. So, you have only to strike, Van Helsing. I will not resist.

Dracula moves Van Helsing's hand, placing the point of the dagger over his own heart.

DRACULA - Your move, Professor.

Van Helsing hesitates, backs away, then suddenly, forcefully, lunges toward the vampire. Dracula catches him and twists him around, cracking the bones of his good arm with an audible snap. Van Helsing collapses.

DRACULA - So disappointing, Professor. I wish you to remain here, alive but powerless, for the time being. I take a new bride this night. You will give her the gift of your blood, sanctified through my veins. Then you will perish. This is my mercy.

He begins to feed on Van Helsing.

2-4E: The Lower Catacombs

Jack sits with the body of Lucy draped across his lap. She appears to be dead. The stake is gone, having been taken by Father Shaugnessy. Quincy Morris appears.

QUINCY - Dr. Seward.

He sees Lucy's body.

QUINCY - I'm sorry things had to happen this way. Where's the priest?

SEWARD - He has gone to bury the bodies of two children. He destroyed them. He had to.

QUINCY - Is she dead?

SEWARD - I wish to take her away from here, bury her in sacred ground. If Van Helsing were here, he would tell me to puncture her heart and remove her head.

QUINCY - You should leave now. You've done what you came to do.

SEWARD - Why did you allow me to enter this place?

QUINCY - I couldn't stand to see her walking around like that. It's unholy, this whole business. I'm gonna suffer for it in Hell, Dr. Seward.

SEWARD - If there is a God, and if he is merciful, then we shall all be tried as madmen, not as criminals.

QUINCY - You best be on your way now. If anyone else catches you down here, it's your own life.

SEWARD - I would be left alone, Mr. Morris. Please.

Quincy kneels and lifts Lucy's face, taking a final look.

QUINCY - It's too bad, angel.

Quincy rises and exits.

SEWARD - I'm sorry, Lucy.

Lucy moves. Her arm rises to embrace Seward.

LUCY - Jack...

SEWARD - Lucy?

LUCY - I need you, Jack. You are so warm. Hold me closer, love.

SEWARD - Yes, Lucy.

Seward gives in to her embrace. She bares his neck and kisses it, preparing to bite. He smiles as her teeth make contact. Lights fade. In the darkness, there is no scream.

2-4F: The Altar Chamber (Finale)

*R*enfield *leads Mina to the altar and sits her down. She is now dressed in a shroud-like gown. Van Helsing is crumpled on the ground nearby.*

RENFIELD - As long as I am here, you can be sure that no harm will befall you. But things are about to change. Soon, you will belong to him. There will be no more debates and letters to the editor. A pity, as I quite enjoyed them. I have kept a file, you know.

Mina sits on the altar, to weak to go further.

MINA - Mr. Renfield, will you please get me out of here...

RENFIELD - I would if I could, dear woman. Please know that this is not my wish. I would write an entirely different ending for you, but I don't have any say in these matters now. My part is nearly done.

Mina tries to stand up but falters

RENFIELD - Please, don't try to run. You have very little blood. The Master will be here soon. He will replenish you from his own veins. You will fall away, and you will be reborn.

MINA - No, I don't believe in this...

RENFIELD - You soon will. I am awfully sorry. It has been an honor to know you as you once were. You and I have a lot in common. We don't fit in. Perhaps in this new order we shall take our rightful place. I don't know. He is here now. I must say goodbye.

Dracula has appeared. Renfield takes one last look at Mina. He exits. Dracula goes to Mina and lifts her to her feet. He gazes directly at her. She turns her face away.

DRACULA - Mina.

MINA - I'm still dreaming.

DRACULA - You are about to enter a new life. You will drink of my blood, as I drink the last of yours. We will be one. Look into my eyes.

MINA - No!

DRACULA - Do not resist me. I can destroy you with only a touch.

MINA - Then destroy me...

Mina begins to mouth words, silently, to herself.

DRACULA - Are you praying, my child?

She does not answer, but continues talking silently.

DRACULA - (*more forcefully*) Are you praying?

MINA - I must be.

DRACULA - You have great strength. In the world to come, you will have a place of power, very near to me. You must look into my eyes now.

MINA - (*refusing to look at him*) You must destroy me.

DRACULA - You say these words, but I detect the truth behind them. You have strength of will, and I can give you power. *This* power you are feeling now, power to press your desires and your will upon whomever you may please. (*He finally catches Mina's eyes*) There. I have your gaze at last. No one has ever resisted me this long.

Mina is now locked in a gaze with the vampire. He bares his chest and draws a long, sharp nail down it, drawing a line of blood. Mina opens her mouth, and he presses her head against his chest. She begins to drink. Dracula seeks out her neck as she clamors again for the blood flowing from his chest. This tryst is suddenly interrupted by a sharp light, and the entrance of Quincy, Shaughnessy, and Renfield.

RENFIELD - Be careful!

SHAUGNESSY - Dear God!

Mina draws away from the vampire and screams. There is a flash, and Dracula is gone. Mina cries out, and begins wiping the blood from her face, choking.

MINA - No! NO!!

RENFIELD - It's all right. I came back. It's all right!

Mina faints away.

SHAUGNESSY - Where has he gone?

RENFIELD - He could be anywhere.

VAN HELSING - *(from the ground)* She must have blood.

RENFIELD - *(examining Mina's face)* - We may be too late.

QUINCY - What should we do?

RENFIELD - If she slips from us now, she will rise again as one of them.

VAN HELSING - *(coughing and sitting up)* I am here.

QUINCY - Van Helsing.

VAN HELSING - I am here. And my case. *(cough)* The transfusion apparatus.

SHAUGNESSY - Miraculous fortune. I will supply my own blood, Van Helsing.

VAN HELSING - You and I need our strength, Father. You are old, and I have been nearly drained. Mr. Morris, it seems you have an opportunity to redeem yourself.

RENFIELD - Then allow me to do the procedure. I believe I know how. Just let me bar the door. It may slow his entry.

As Renfield goes to the door, Dracula appears very suddenly.

DRACULA - You were mistaken to think I had gone away. I have hidden myself from your weak senses. You, Renfield, have betrayed me.

RENFIELD - I know, your excellency. I was not ready to see her die. Forgive me.

DRACULA - You are a foolish insect. You are nothing!

Dracula tears at Renfield, who issues a blood-curdling scream and drops to the floor, a lifeless heap.

DRACULA - Go ahead. Refill her veins, my friends. It will make her stronger. But she will follow me. You display a superficial courage. I will indulge your desire for a fight. You have but to find me.

He leaves. There is a sound of a door being closed and bolted. They are trapped.

VAN HELSING - Mr. Renfield...

SHAUGNESSY - He is breathing.

RENFIELD - I have but a moment, Father.

SHAUGNESSY - Do you want to make your confession?

RENFIELD - There's no time. Take the black bag. Pierce my arm with that needle, and give my blood to Miss Mina.

SHAUGNESSY - I will try.

RENFIELD - Quickly, Father. She must have living blood.

QUINCY - I think I can help you, Father.

Quincy brings the apparatus. Father Shaugnessy quietly recites the Lord's Prayer as the transfusion is given. Van Helsing looks on weakly. There is silence, only the quiet prayer of Shaugnessy. There is a brief passage of time indicated by a shift of light.

SHAUGNESSY - You have given enough, Mr. Renfield.

RENFIELD - No. All that I have. Please. I will be gone in another breath.

Mina begins to move. She looks at Renfield.

RENFIELD - Miss Murray. You and I shall be linked together. My blood, your body. It's like marriage, or like ...reincarnation, or more like ...salvation...

He is dead.

QUINCY - That's all, Father. He's gone.

SHAUGNESSY - We need to make a circle. I have the consecrated host.

He rises and makes a circle from the crumbled host.

SHAUGNESSY - Bring her into the circle. The vampire cannot enter into it.

VAN HELSING - I am not so sure.

SHAUGNESSY - You have no faith. But I have. So did that poor, wretched man. So too does this woman, I think.

Quincy guides Mina into the circle. She sits within it.

QUINCY - You're all right now.

MINA - Jonathan?

QUINCY - No. Quincy.

MINA - I thought Jonathan had come to me...

QUINCY - Father, we need to get her out of here.

There is a sound of a heavy door opening and closing.

VAN HELSING - Someone is coming.

SHAUGNESSY - Let's stay quiet, and pray.

Lucy appears behind them. She is carrying the bloodied stake.

LUCY - Father...

SHAUGNESSY - Dear God...

LUCY - You left this behind.

SHAUGNESSY - You cannot enter the circle.

LUCY - Did you not mean to nail *me* to the ground with this? You should finish what has been started, Father. You have destroyed my children...

SHAUGNESSY - They were not yours.

LUCY - You have destroyed my children...

SHAUGNESSY - By all the powers of heaven, I cast you away...

He sprinkles the holy water. Lucy shrinks from it.

MINA - Lucy...

Lucy looks to Mina. There is a moment of strange recognition.

LUCY - Mina?

Lucy effortlessly enters the circle and kneels next to Mina. She drops the stake on the ground beside her.

LUCY - Mina! How has this happened to you? He promised me no harm would ever come to you. He promised.

Shaugnessy draws his knife. He looks to Quincy, motioning him to do the same. He begins to advance on Lucy. Dracula appears in front of them, between the circle and the front of the stage, quite suddenly.

DRACULA - Stay away from her!

QUINCY - My God...

DRACULA - I gave you the chance to run. You remained here. There will be no more chances.

Quincy and Shaugnessy back away from the vampire, moving slowly upstage. Dracula turns away and disappears. An instant later, he emerges from behind the two, an impossible shift from one place to another. As he speaks the following line, he closes in on the two, who retreat to the circle.

DRACULA - *(holding all in his gaze)* Follow me into the catacombs. It will be an excellent contest. And when I win this game, believe me, I will not kill you quickly. You will linger in such pain as you never dreamed of. So follow. Follow...

Lucy suddenly takes the stake and lunges upward toward Dracula, impaling him. Dracula screams and clutches at the stake.

SHAUGNESSY - The knives! Now!

Shaugnessy and Quincy attack Dracula with their consecrated knives.

VAN HELSING - Father, for God's sake, be careful!

The vampire is reaching for Shaugnessy. Quincy pushes the Father out of harm's way. He plunges his knife near to the vampire's heart. Dracula takes Quincy by the throat. They are locked in a mortal embrace. Quincy dies, and presently, the vampire falls to the ground.

Lucy goes to Dracula, still just barely alive.

LUCY - We are destroyed.

DRACULA - Yes. It was well done. Now lay beside me. Together, we will fall to dust.

He slumps forward, nearly gone.

VAN HELSING - Mr. Morris...

SHAUGNESSY - He is dead. I must give absolution...

MINA - Lucy...

Lucy goes to Mina and places her own cold hand on Mina's.

LUCY - I fought him. For you. That must be my soul...

Mina embraces her. Lucy gently pushes her away.

LUCY - You should go now. There is no hope for me.

MINA - I will stay here...

LUCY - No. I do not wish for you to see what must be done to me. These men must destroy my body. Please go.

MINA - No, Lucy. I will stay. Until this is done.

Lucy goes to the body of Dracula and lies beside it. The lights fade.

Mina steps forward into an area only half lit. She speaks.

MINA - I have left London, unable to face the inquest into the deaths at the abbey. I have left this journal with Father Shaugnessy, in the hopes that these words will find the right person. I must go in search of Jonathan. I entertain no hope that he has survived. And yet, I must know what has become of him. I must know all I can about the forces that took him from me, that took Miriam and Lucy as well. I must find the source. I must understand it. I must know.

Epilogue: The Castle in Transylvania

Arthur Holmwood has arrived at the ancestral home of Dracula, and enters much as Harker did so long ago. Harker now sits on a chair on the upstage platform . The box has been moved off of the platform, just downstage of it, standing in for a table. Arthur enters stage right.

ARTHUR - Hello. Is anyone here?

A voice emerges from the darkness, then a shadowy figure. He stands atop the center platform, his bearing that of a nobleman.

HARKER - Arthur Holmwood. I suppose I must call you Lord Godalming.

ARTHUR - I can't see you.

HARKER - I am here. Look closely.

We clearly see Harker, now at home in his new domain, pale but with a bearing that indicates unspeakable strength.

HARKER - To what do I owe this honor, Godalming?

ARTHUR - The Order of the Reckoning. Our numbers are still strong. Things didn't work out for Dracula.

HARKER - Yes. We felt his passing, even here.

ARTHUR - But there are many who still believe in our plan. Everything is in place for us to begin a new society. We only need someone to lead us.

HARKER - Do you honor me with an invitation?

ARTHUR - You have royal blood.

HARKER - And such a short time ago, I was your ignorant pawn. How fortunes do shift.

ARTHUR - How could we know what fate held for you? But we rejoice in it now.

Three more figures have appeared; Anja. Katja, and Karena. They are slowly closing in on Arthur.

HARKER - How very touching. I do hope you will stay for supper.

ARTHUR - It is kind of you to offer it.

HARKER - Think nothing of it. Ladies, please attend to our guest.

The three vampire brides draw closer to Arthur.

HARKER - These are my brides, Holmwood. The blood of Nosferatu thrives in their veins as well.

KARENA - We like him.

ANJA - Very much.

KATJA - So strong.

HARKER - As to your Order of the Reckoning, I wish them every good fortune. However, I have plans here. I hope I do not disappoint. I am glad you could join us. We've been looking forward to your arrival. We've been hungry.

ANJA - Very hungry.

KATJE & KARENA - *(Overlapping)* Very hungry.

Holmwood is overwhelmed by the vampire brides. They force him on his back onto the table and gather around him. His screams resound along with the laughter of Harker, the newest heir to the throne of Nosferatu.

Curtain

END OF PLAY

Notes to the Second Edition

F irst Version Premiere Cast

Originally written as a three-act under play the title DRACULA: BLOOD OF NOSFERATU, it premiered on October 24, 1997 at the Lights! Camera! Action! Theater, located at the Disney MGM Studios. (Now Disney's Hollywood Studios) The production was directed by Jim Mundy and Darryl Pickett, and was produced by Richard Spiller. The cast was as follows:

Count Dracula - Colin S. Coughenour

Professor Abraham Van Helsing - Ken Harrington

Mina Murray - Stewart Hamilton-Frank

Lucy Westenra - Katherine R. Phillips

Miriam Westenra – Patsy Puckett

Jonathan Harker – Jim Mundy

Thomas Renfield - L. Michael Mundell

Dr. Jack Seward - Eric Sweetman

Father Shaugnessy - T.J. Wollard

Arthur Holmwood (*Lord Godalming*) - Jason Hairel

Quincy Morris - Gabriel McLeod

Simon – Shane Rhodes

Harriet – Chelsea Rhodes

Karena - Debbie Sussman

BLOOD OF NOSFERATU: A PLAY IN TWO ACTS

Anja - Sami Nadeau

Katja - Amy Brate

A Porter - Philip G. Faiss

Jenkins - Philip G. Faiss

Parsons - Ray Mowers

Mr. Preston – Ray Mowers

The roles of the Porter and Mr. Preston were deleted from the revised version. Preston's part was largely absorbed by Renfield, and the Porter disappeared when we lost the train sequence. The creators of those roles are nonetheless much appreciated for their contributions.

Origins and Ambitions

This play came about when I was working at Walt Disney World, and participating in a club known as S.T.A.G.E. (Society for Theater Arts, Growth, and Expression). We were a club comprised of Disney World employees, who are known as Cast Members. Our board suggested that for the following October, we put on the 1924 Hamilton Dean/John Balderston play *Dracula*. It's a frequently performed staple thanks to the man most associated with the title role, Bela Lugosi. He originated the role on stage and reprised it in the iconic 1931 Universal film. Both play and movie are similarly stage bound, with dialogue describing key moments instead of showing them. I love the film, but felt the play had become a stodgy artifact. I boasted that I could write a better one, and I was given a year to make good on it, with no guarantee that my efforts would automatically be accepted.

in October, 1996, we presented my three-act effort to fellow Cast Members, family, and friends. It ran nearly three and a half hours. I had stuffed the play full of characters, settings, and subplots. It was overloaded with nods to Bram Stoker's novel, as well as F.W. Murnau's 1922 silent film *Nosferatu*, and Wernor Herzog's 1979 remake. I also drew on my love for Hammer horror, and my familiarity with many film versions of the story. As a result, the play was a self-indulgent marathon, asking a lot of actors and audience. I had not killed any darlings, nor left any of my ideas out. It had compelling scenes, but it was exhausting to sit through.

Given the popularity of the subject matter, and the large cast, we considered it a reasonable success. But I knew it needed to be trimmed down and spruced up. A year later, I paid a self-publishing service and put out a slightly revised version of the premiere script. To my astonishment, I received a lot of requests for performance rights.

The work had been rushed to the marketplace. But still, within a few years, it had been staged in Texas, Oklahoma, New York City, Oxford, even Mexico

BLOOD OF NOSFERATU: A PLAY IN TWO ACTS

City, where an eager student had translated it into Spanish. I even learned that some unauthorized productions had taken place. I encouraged producers and directors to share with me any observations and lessons learned, and I particularly wanted to know which scenes they were most inclined to omit or shorten. My unwieldy play got work-shopped over time and across continents.

In 2012, I completed an extensive revision that brought three acts down to two. I telescoped and compressed many scenes, and added a few enhancements along the way. In 2018, I received a request for performing rights from a group in Enniscorthy, Ireland, wanting to stage the three-act version. I agreed on the condition that they instead test drive my two-act revision. Throughout their production, I was given lots of feedback, with photos and video, and that has led to even more tweaks. This edition benefits from their experience, and I consider it the final authorized text.

For all the improvements, this is still what I would call an early effort. I left much of the original text intact, and it remains the naive, overambitious work of a young writer trying too hard to impress. But now, it is a more practical and achievable play for companies able to summon a large enough cast.

What follows are notes and suggestions that should prove helpful for anyone bringing this version to their local audiences and communities.

Production Notes and Nudges

Most of the suggestions below come from successful ideas implemented along the play's decades-long journey. Key to a successful production is simplicity. We learned in that original production the hard way: Don't build a lot of realistic, heavy scenery. With the many settings, and the alternating back and forth between locations, you don't want your audience to wait in silence while an ornate parlor or an imposing castle interior is assembled. Even if you fill the downtime with appropriately eerie music, the constant breaks quickly grow tedious. In order to keep the pace moving, it is important to move from scene to scene with cinematic speed. The key is in a versatile and simple unit set.

Swiftly Shifting Scenery

In order to facilitate the large number of rapid scene changes, *Blood of Nosferatu* should be performed without traditional scenery. The furniture, props, and especially costumes, will do the visual work. I recommend a set comprised of a bare stage with a raised platform occupying a portion of the upstage area. Shadows or projections may be used against the backdrop to help establish setting and mood. Lightweight chairs, small end tables and props are carried on and off by the cast. Don't be afraid to play the changes in full view. Characters who are present at the top of a scene may usually bring on their own chairs.

Scenes may be played on either end of the lower stage and the upper platform, and both may be occupied simultaneously. By raising lights on one area and lowering them on another, the action can shift between two places without the need for much pause. Transitions should be made as quickly and smoothly as possible. Have at least one rehearsal for just this.

On the upstage platform is an oblong wooden box. By changing its coverings, it is used to represent beds and an altar where indicated. When uncovered, it may be sat on. It should be strong but light enough that it can be shifted long-side-out or short-side-out with minimal fuss. This edition describes moves that have proven effective in suggesting many scenes and settings, with minimal fuss.

Costumes as Spectacle

Though the set is simple, the costumes are your chance to leave an impression of lavish spectacle. Let your costumes be your scenery, in essence. Make them as detailed and elaborate as your company's wardrobe can manage. (Though simple costumes have also worked very well.) Consider color pallets and styles appropriate to the characters, their status, and their inner states over the course of the story. Though the play contains a lot of dialogue, it is great to let wardrobe tell much of the story visually. That said, keep in mind that there are frequent costume changes, and dramatic action. Keep the costumes comfortable, flexible, and amenable to quick changes.

On a related note, makeup should be simple and transitions from living to undead should not require a long time in the makeup chair, as this won't often be possible. The nature of the venue can have an impact. I like intimate spaces that keep the audience close to the players. As to special makeup, Dracula's look should be unique, likely the most carefully designed and applied. The script suggests that he be vulpine, with facial hair that suggests a wolf-like appearance and nature. In early scenes, he is presented as old and seemingly weak, though as he feeds, he can be made to appear stronger and more powerful. Lighting can aid in this. The cape with bat-like cowl is traditional, but perhaps cliche. Feel free to play with other looks. Make him unworldly and ferocious. Finally, I caution that fake fangs can sabotage the best portrayal of Dracula, or any other vampire character. They draw attention to their presence by garbling speech, and don't contribute to natural expression. My experience suggests that they are best done without. Let words and actions convey menace. Everyone knows what biting a neck means. I know of custom fangs that are molded to the performer's teeth, and look good up close in movies, but in. this case, the terror of the victim and the voraciousness of the vampire are what will really leave an impact.

Scene Specific Moments and Other Notes

The opening Prelude described at the top of Act One is optional, and inspired by the fact that the Renfield of the original cast had the talent of getting out of an ungimmicked straight jacket. Other productions have used commercially available easy-escape versions, but this is an avoidable expense, and the rest of the show doesn't call for any such prop. There are many other ways to establish mood and atmosphere before the show begins.

The lecture attendees Parsons and Jenkins can be doubled by the actors in the principle roles of Arthur Holmwood and Quincy. (Or you may prefer to cast eager house staff, as they remain in the house, heard but not necessarily seen.)

For the moment when Renfield takes out his sack of bugs and eats them, we discovered that convincing stage replicas can be made with bodies comprised of dried plums, with wings cut from dark-colored fruit leather, and perhaps a crisp layer of rice cracker or similar for a bit of crunch, and some syrup to ooze out. Be sure to have your Renfield bite the bugs mid-body for maximum "ew" factor. Make them large enough, and your performer can even wriggle them convincingly before tucking in.

The startling moment in the finale when Dracula appears at the edge of the stage apron and then instantly appears on the upstage altar was achieved by having the actor in the role of Arthur don a cape and hairpiece that gave him a reasonable likeness to Dracula. He hid at the edge of the stage nearest the audience and emerged with a burst of light and a shock chord from the audio. The lights then went down on him and immediately to Dracula on the upstage altar. Dracula leapt from there to his rivals below. The moment was quick and effective. Keep it simple.

The author encourages diverse casting, especially in regards to race or gender. Take the opportunity to reflect your community and bring people into your arts scene who may not have felt welcome or inclined before. The new talent you bring will strengthen and broaden your theater's reach and versatility, and expand your audience.

BLOOD OF NOSFERATU: A PLAY IN TWO ACTS

The author has composed a suite of music and atmospheres to accompany specific moments in the play. These may be found at the Resources section of the page dedicated to this play at www.odsmil.com. Productions that have secured performance rights may use these tracks, but are under no obligation to do so.

This play requires a great deal of work and commitment. This will pay off in a memorable audience experience, and a sense of real camaraderie for the company. The author is always keen to hear how your production went.

Above all, keep energy high, and keep the pace brisk.

About the Author

D arryl Pickett is a professional writer and content creator for the theme park industry. A former Walt Disney Imagineer, and ongoing story consultant, he stumbled into that industry by way of also being an actor, singer, and songwriter. He decided to add novelist to his restless resume in 2012, with his first full-length fiction, *The Secret Feast of Father Christmas.*

Darryl has been creating original theatrical works for over two decades. His most recent play, *Analog,* is a time-portal homage to vinyl records and J.S. Bach. He is presently collaborating on *Trollop,* a rock operetta inspired by Daniel Defoe's Moll Flanders.

His most recent novel, *Shark City Harbor,* is his first foray into crime and suspense, prompted by a vacation he took to both Manhattan and Martha's Vineyard. He enjoyed the journey of writing it so much, he is already at work on its sequel.